The Tellier and
Brunelle Families
1665 - 2009

AN AMERICAN STORY

The Tellier and
Brunelle Families
1665 - 2009

AN AMERICAN STORY

J. Robert Brunelle

Outskirts Press, Inc.
Denver, Colorado

For
Mom and Dad
Who gave me a sense of family

The opinions expressed in this manuscript are solely the opinions of the author and do not represent the opinions or thoughts of the publisher. The author has represented and warranted full ownership and/or legal right to publish all the materials in this book.

AN AMERICAN STORY
The Tellier and Brunelle Families 1665 - 2009
All Rights Reserved.
Copyright © 2010 J. Robert Brunelle
v3.0

This book may not be reproduced, transmitted, or stored in whole or in part by any means, including graphic, electronic, or mechanical without the express written consent of the publisher except in the case of brief quotations embodied in critical articles and reviews.

Outskirts Press, Inc.
http://www.outskirtspress.com

ISBN: 978-1-4327-5615-4

Outskirts Press and the "OP" logo are trademarks belonging to Outskirts Press, Inc.

PRINTED IN THE UNITED STATES OF AMERICA

Table of Contents

Author's Preface vii

Acknowledgements ix

Prologue xiii

Chapter 1.   Beginnings 1642-1665 1

Chapter 2.   Soldiers in New France, 1665-1668 7

Chapter 3.   Jean LeTellier 1668-1704 13

Chapter 4.   The Tellier Family in the Agricultural Age, 1704 to the 1880's 21

Chapter 5.   The Limousin, Beaufort, Brunelle Family, 1668 to 1872 27

Chapter 6.   The Arsene Brunelle Family 1872-1920's 31

Chapter 7.   The Joseph Tellier Family 1884-1923 47

Chapter 8.   A Union of the Descendents 1923 - 1930 69

Chapter 9.   The Great Depression 1929-1939 75

Chapter 10. A New Beginning 1938-1939 89

Chapter 11. WORLD WAR II 1939 – 1945 95

Chapter 12. The Post War Years, 1946 – 1952 105

Chapter 13. My Military Service Years - 1952 to 1956 115

Chapter 14. Life in the Long Island City
             House 1950 – 1970 127

Chapter 15. A Decade of Personal
             Change 1959 – 1968 131

Chapter 16. From the Author's Perspective
             1970 – 1997 141

Chapter 17. Life After Retirement 1998 – 2006 157

Chapter 18. Harvey and Alice Brunelle's Grandchildren
             and Great Grandchildren - 2009 173

Epilogue 179

Tellier And Brunelle Family Tree 183

Photographs 184

Author's Preface

The story you are about to read is a true story, it is not historical fiction. It begins in the middle of the 17th century, and continues up to the present time, the opening of the 21st century. The story commences when two young men, French soldiers of the King in the same regiment, are sent across the ocean to a new world, New France. Their King was Louis XIV, "The Sun King," and the two men were my first maternal and paternal ancestors in the Americas.

The story will continue with their lives in the New World, and the lives of each succeeding generation, down to my own. It represents a total of 337 years, counting from when the soldiers both disembarked in New France in 1665, to the present year of 2002.

My mother, born Marie Antionette Alice Tellier in Quebec, Canada, is the tenth generation of one of the soldiers. My father, Herve Brunelle, born in Manville, Rhode Island, represents the ninth generation of the second soldier. In 1924, exactly 259 years after the soldiers arrived in New France, my parents, direct linear descendents of each soldier, were united in marriage, thereby creating a single bloodline for the descendents that follow.

This story is the history of these two families, the Telliers and the Brunelles. I realize there are those who might justifiably ask: Why do we need another family history? I would respond that this story is more than just a family genealogical study. It is essentially a slice of history of three great nations in which the French people have resided. It is the history of a people who have maintained their heritage, language and culture over the centuries to the present time.

If one travels the villages and towns of New England today, he will find entire communities that still speak the French language at home, in church and at work and commerce. The French language and culture, still practiced in the Province of Quebec, Canada, was carried and maintained between France and New France, and then transplanted to the United States in the great French-Canadian migration of the late 19th and early 20th centuries. The history of these people is the history of our nation, not only since this great migration, but since the early struggles between the English and the French prior to the American Revolution.

Numerous novels have been written about various periods of French history in the Americas. I have long dreamed of writing, as have many others, the "Great American Novel." Unfortunately, I believe I lack one of the necessary ingredients for this endeavor: imagination. The beauty in writing this family history, from a personal perspective, is that I don't need imagination. I only require the facts and the stories of my ancestors. My imagination could never have risen to the heights of family reality. I could never have fictionalized such a story.

The travails, joys and sorrows, triumphs and tragedies experienced by my ancestors is representative of millions of our nation's peoples, and in this sense universal. In writing of my family, I am writing the history of our nation. One must think of the story that follows as not merely a personal family story, but as a small contribution to the overall history of North America.

Acknowledgements

As indicated by the dedication, I must first acknowledge my parents' contribution to this book, Throughout his life, my father patiently answered any questions I posed to him about his family and his early life. Though basically a quiet modest man, as was his father, he was also a thoughtful and considerate man and clearly indulged my youthful and often insistent questions.

My mother, thankfully, has enjoyed extraordinary longevity and is at this writing 98 years young, and still clear of mind. To her I owe the numerous recollections of her family, going back almost a century. Her ability to remember portions of her life as far back as 1906, when she was three years old, is truly remarkable. These recollections are the basis for almost one-third of my maternal family history represented in the three-century timespan of this book.

To my sister Connie Gil, who has been our mother's caregiver and companion for many years, thanks for all the good care you have given our mother. I'm sure it contributed substantially to her longevity.

To my wife Marta I owe everything from Internet research, word processing of the manuscript, proofreading, and all the functions you might receive from an editor. Beyond this, however, I am grateful to her for her untiring support and patience. Her own family heritage goes back a good 2,500 years to ancient Greece, and makes my own ancestry seem miniscule indeed.

I am grateful to my son Christopher, who has always enthusiastically encouraged me to "do it, Dad," "it" being this book. In addition, his oral history videotapes of his grandmother have been an invaluable source and inspiration for my efforts. Also, thank you is due both to Chris and my daughter Lesley for the great Christmas gift of my own video camera. This camcorder has enabled me to visually record actual original sites in Canada, New England and New York where this story took place.

Many other family members have aided me in my family research. To my uncle Ernest Villeneuve, who himself lived to 98 years, I owe much genealogy information for the two generations that came before me. For information about my immediate family in the 1930's and '40's, I am indebted to my brother Normand. For information about our common grandfather's story, I am greatly indebted to my cousin Rene Tellier, who is himself writing a memoir of the family. Other cousins who supplied much appreciated information are Robert Tellier (Rene's brother), brothers Gene and Norman Peloquin, Patricia Severson and last, but certainly not least, Vivian Brunelle.

Finally, from a personal point of view, I must credit two more individuals. For spiritual and historical inspiration I am indebted to two of America's most famous authors, one a Pulitzer Prize novelist, one a prize-winning historian. To Willa Cather, the early 20th century novelist, I am especially indebted for her body of work portraying the lives of America's early pioneers. Particular inspiration is derived from her fictional biography of the real life French priest Jean Baptiste Lamy in *Death Comes For The Archbishop*, and also the French Quebec characters in *Shadows on the Rock*.

My historical inspiration comes from Francis Parkman, the 19th century author whose lifelong quest and portrayal of the struggles of the French peoples in North America is told in his numerous history books on the subject. These books are now assembled for the modern reader in two volumes entitled *France and England in North America*.

Both authors, now long since departed, brought the same passion to their works. Cather, the novelist, researched the background of her books like a professional historian; Parkman, though a consummate historian, wrote his books like a professional novelist.

I have attempted, in a modest way, to emulate and combine both of their storytelling techniques. To the reader's good judgment goes the decision as to how well I have succeeded.

✠ Prologue ✠

"The French dominion is a memory of the past; and when we evoke its departed shades, they rise upon us from their graves in strange, romantic guise. again their ghostly campfires seem to burn, and the fitful light is cast around on lord and vassal and black-robed priest, mingled with wild forms of savage warriors, knit in close fellowship on the same stern errand. A boundless vision grown upon us; an untamed continent; vast wastes of forest verdure; mountains silent in primeval sleep, river, lake, and glimmering pool; wilderness oceans mingling with the sky . . . Plumed helmets gleamed in the shade of its forests, priestly vestments in its dens and fastnesses of ancient barbarism. Men steeped in antique learning, pale with the close breath of the cloister, here spent the noon and evening of their lives, ruled savage hordes with a mild, parental sway, and stood serene before the direst shapes of death. Men of courtly nature, heirs to the polish of a far reaching ancestory, here with their dauntless hardihood, put to shame the boldest sons of toil."

by Francis Parkman in
"Pioneers of France in the New World"

CHAPTER 1

Beginnings 1642-1665

His name was Jean Baptiste LeTellier and he was born at a time when his country was on the verge of becoming a world power. Louis XIV had been born in 1638, just four years before Jean's own birth in 1642. Jean's* birthplace was Coutances, a town on the western coast of south Normandy. His[1]* size and appearance are unknown to us, however, by the appearance of many of his male descendants his hair may have been light, his eyes blue, and his build and height above average. Though not typical French characteristics, we must not forget the Viking history of Normandy. In the 800's Norseman warriors began their conquests by raiding French coasts and river valleys. By the 900's, Normans had conquered most of the present Normandy area and adopted the Catholic religion, and the French customs and language.

Jean's father's name was Nicholas LeTellier and his mother's maiden name was Elisabeth Delespine. It is probable that given the agricultural dominance of the area in which he was born, and his latter occupation in adulthood, Jean was born into a small farm family. It is also probable that the family was large, given the Catholic customs of France. This religious custom also had an economic basis, since many children were needed to operate the

---
1 For brevity of text, Jean Baptiste LeTellier will henceforth be referred to by his first name, Jean.

labor intensive small farms. His given name of Jean Baptiste (from John The Baptist) was a common French first name of the times, and reflected the Catholic background of most Frenchmen.

A visit to Coutances today gives one a hint of what Jean would have found in his own time. The most prominent feature, both in 1642 and certainly today, is the 13th century Cathedrale Notre Dame. Among its turrets, spires and slender shafts is an octagonal latern rising 135 feet above the church nave. Although its exact population in Jean's time is not known, it may not have been very different than its present population of approximately 7,500. One still finds Norman-style cottages in the town and countryside, and Jean may well feel at home if he returned today.

From early age Jean would have helped his father Nicholas on the farm and would have received little, if any; schooling. One suspects that Jean was an ambitious young man, since at some point before he reached the age of twenty-one he decided to join the French army. Clearly, remaining a farm boy in a large family would not have held any future for advancing his prospects in life.

Becoming a soldier in the French army was certainly a means to advancement for Jean. Early in his reign, Louis XIV began building up the army to support his increasing military adventures on the European Continent and in New France in the Americas. Jean enlisted in one of the King's premier regiments, the Carignan Regiment. This regiment had already served France with distinction in several wars.

At his enlistment, Jean, not being a literate man, would have made his mark rather than signed his name. Throughout his life Jean appears to have remained illiterate and his distinctive mark (*M*), rather than a simple "X" comes down to us in history, being used later on his various land purchases and sales in New France.

Jean was assigned to the Froment Company and given the "Dit" name of "LaFortune". Since the name LaFortune was to come down to many of Jean's descendants as a surname, as well as the LeTellier surname, it is appropriate at this point to give the reader the meaning and history of "dit" names in the French society of the times.

The French word "dit" translates to "said" or "spoken." It became a French custom, going back to before the 16th century, to give people "dit" names to aid in the positive identification of an individual. A "dit" name was not a nickname, an alias or an aka (also known as). It was a name that was an extension to an existing name, and became part and parcel to the original basic name.

In Jean Baptiste LeTellier's case, the "dit" name given him at the time he enlisted in the French army was "LaFortune." Jean would in essence now be identified as Jean Baptiste LeTellier dit LaFortune. He would still have the same legal surname of LeTellier, but he would now be differentiated from any other LeTelliers in the army by his dit name, LaFortune. We must remember that the French at this period in time had very large families. It was not uncommon for farm families to have more than a dozen children, which often produced enormous numbers of name duplications.

We must also remember that identification numbering assigned by the army to their soldiers, is a relatively modern innovation. The dit names assigned to young men by the French were often taken from an attribute of the man. For example, a large recruit might be assigned the dit name "LaMontagne" which literally translates to "the mountain" man.

This custom of dit names was carried to New France and some families to this day are still using a "double" family name. Such was the case of Jean Baptiste LeTellier dit LaFortune. Some of his subsequent descendents in New France (and then Canada) bear surnames of LeTellier, Tellier, LeTellier-LaFortune and just LaFortune.

LeTellier's dit name, LaFortune, translates to "the chance or the fortune." As faith and irony would have it, Jean's life in New

France did live up to the English meaning of his dit name.

Although LeTellier is not a particularly common French name, it happened that at the time of Jean's enlistment in the army, Louis XIV's minister, who handled most military matters, was a man named Michel LeTellier. It is very probable that the recruitment officers would have noticed this surname coincidence. It may even have contributed to Jean being recruited into one of the King's premier regiments. At the very least, the coincidence would not have hurt the chances of a young farmer getting into a good regiment.

This author is not aware of any family relationship between the two men, and given their greatly different stations in life, it is doubtful that there was a close, if any, relationship. However, the name coincidence is interesting and the reader may find a short biography of Michel LeTellier germane to Jean's newly-chosen occupation of soldier.

Shortly after becoming king, Louis XIV decided that his monarchy would be a personal one, and that he would exercise and retain all powers to himself. He did, however, surround himself throughout his long reign with a few able ministers and advisors. Two of the most important of these men were a father and son named Michel LeTellier (1603-1685) and Francois-Michel LeTellier (1639-1691), respectively. Michel LeTellier was one of the wealthiest and most powerful officials in France and served the King as Minister of War. He groomed and educated his son to serve as his replacement and by 1665, (Jean's first or second year in the army), the King had granted the son Francois the right to handle all the duties of his father's office. The younger LeTellier was to receive the official title of Minister of War after his father's death and subsequently remodeled the French army. He comes down to us as one of France's and Europe's most important figures in 17th century military history. More information on these LeTellier's influence on Jean's life will follow in Chapter 2.

In 1663 the commercial company of New France had been disbanded and Louis XIV made New France a French colony. Due to the difficulties the new colony was having with their neighbors (the British and the Iroquois indians who generally sided with the British), the King decided to send his entire Carignan regiment to the new colony. In the spring of 1665 Jean Baptiste LeTellier, a 23 year old French soldier, and over 1,000 of his regimental companions boarded ships in La Rochelle and sailed for North America.

An Atlantic crossing in the late 17th century took approximately two months and the average ships in use in this period were on the order of 100 feet long and 30 feet wide. Jean's ship was a 250 ton royal ship called the St. Sebastian. Jean and his regimental companions would probably have occupied the hold of the ship, which ran the entire length of the ship. The men would have slept next to each other on military-supplied mattresses or bedding. Also stowed in the hold would have been provisions and water for the soldiers and ship's crew. Live animals, cattle, pigs, etc. were commonly carried on shipboard and killed for meals in the transatlantic crossing.

The officers may have occupied narrow cabins as available on the particular ship. The only air available was from small portholes and hatches in the ship's deck. One can imagine the smell that accumulated in a two-month period from men, animals, and latrine pots. Due to the primitive conditions and lack of proper diets, it was not uncommon for sickness to develop in the crossing. It is estimated that in the 1660's, approximately ten percent of the transatlantic passengers between France and New France died in the crossing. In Jean's regiment, 20 soldiers died during the crossing and 130 others were too ill to disembark on their own when the ship reached Quebec. Jean's ship disembarked in New France on June 19, 1665, and Jean Baptiste LeTellier dit LaFortune was to begin a new life in a new world.

CHAPTER 2

Soldiers in New France, 1665-1668

It is at this point in my ancestor's story that I will introduce one of Jean's regimental companions, a soldier named Hilaire Limousin dit Beaufort. Hilaire[2]* is my first paternal ancestor in the Americas and with his story begins the other half of this family history, the Brunelle half. [3]**

Just as in Jean LeTellier dit LaFortune's case, my ancestor Hilaire also had a dit name. The name was Beaufort, hence Hilaire Limousin was given the last name Limousin dit Beaufort. Since "beau" in French translates to attractive and "fort" translates to strong, Hilaire may have been both handsome and strong.

Hilaire was born in 1633 in Poitiers, France. His parents' names were Pierre Limousin and Isabella Fradin. Since I am not confident that I can assume much about Hilaire's life in France, it is appropriate that I begin Hilaire's story with his disembarkation in New France in 1665. Both Hilaire's and Jean's stories will be combined for the three year period 1665 to 1668. Since they were both in the French army in this period, it is reasonable to assume that their lives would have been substantially similar.

---

2 * Again, as with Jean, for brevity of text, Hilaire Limousin dit Beaufort will be referred to by his first name, Hilaire.
3 ** My paternal line surname evolved and changed in subsequent generations. This evolution will be covered in Chapter 5.

By 1665 the French army was one of the best and most powerful armies in the world. The LeTellier ministers, Father Michel and son Francois Michel, who was also known as the Marquis de Louvois, had transformed Louis XIV's army into the most modern and progressive army in Europe. Jean and Hilaire, and their battle-experienced Carignan regiment would have been the beneficiaries of the LeTellier's military reforms and decisions made in their capacity as Ministers of War.

Additionally, Jean and Hilaire's very presence in New France would have been the result of the Ministers' recommendations and decision to send the entire Carignan regiment overseas. Of course, the King retained for himself all final decisions in matters of state, but it is historically recorded that he placed complete trust in the LeTelliers.

Jean, Hilaire and their regiment would have benefited from numerous other military decisions by the LeTelliers. Many new technologies and policies were introduced under their tenure. In the area of military hardware, they introduced the new socket bayonets and the important new flintlock type muskets. Realizing that armies are dependent on supply, they established the first quartermaster general department. Their reforms in this area established the first effective military logistics and began the foundations for today's modern logistics.

They also experimented with new techniques and maneuvers for battle. Concluding that new weapons made it necessary to reduce the depth of battlefield formations, they had adopted the concept of linear warfare. French troops were drilled and trained to deploy from a column into a line and to advance in lines of three ranks. The soldiers were trained to advance in unison, and also to fire their muskets in unison. The LeTellier's progressive reforms were eventually recognized and followed by the rest of Europe's armies.

At the time of the introduction of the 1,000-man Carignan regiment to New France, there were approximately 3,000 inhabitants in the entire French colony. The greatest population concentrations would have been in the Montreal and Quebec areas. Montreal had been founded in 1642, just 23 years before the regiments arrived. Quebec City had been founded in 1608, 77 years before they arrived.

Outside of these two areas, New France was still basically little more than fur trading posts, military garrisons and stockades, missionary houses and small farms. These farms were narrowly laid out in rows, perpendicular to the St. Lawrence River. Local stockades and fortifications were used by the farmers and soldiers as protection from hostile indians. The earliest settlement in Montreal and in Quebec City were each surrounded by protective fortifications. New France was in this period very much as Frances Parkman poetically describes in the "Prologue ". . . an untamed continent; vast wastes of forests. . .mountains silent in primeval sleep, river, lake and glimmering pool."

The introduction of the Carignan regiment represented a 33% increase in the total population of New France and surely increased the colony's security. The regiment's soldiers would have been dispersed to the two major towns, Montreal and Quebec, and also to the various forts and outposts throughout the colony.

Despite serious difficulties with the Iroquois indians, Jean's and Hilaire's tour of duty in New France was probably relatively uneventful. The collision between the French colony and the rival colonies of England in New York and New England had not as yet developed. This rivalry was not to begin in earnest until around 1700 and culminated in the French and Indian War of 1756 through 1763.

As a result of the Catholic Church's missionary efforts in New France which began in the 16th century, the French had by 1665 succeeded in gaining the trust and alliance of the Huron and Algonquin tribes. Many indians were nominally converted to Christianity by the Franciscan and Jesuit missionary priests. The Iroquois and their Indian Confederation were traditional enemies of the Hurons and the Algonquins, and this further contributed to their general animosity with the French. The French, in turn, used this preexisting indian rivalry to strengthen their mutually advantageous alliance with the Hurons and the Algonquins.

One of the earliest serious battles with the Iroquois occurred in 1609 when the French explorer, Samuel de Champlain, joined a war party of Algonquins against their Iroquois enemies. Leaving the town of Quebec and going through Sorel on the south shore of the St. Lawrence River, they proceeded south on the waters of the Richelieu River. Their southward journey brought them to the lake which was later to be named after Champlain. They continued toward the area where the old Fort Ticonderoga now stands in New York. At this point, they encountered a band of Iroquois indians and indian-style tree-to-tree battle ensued.

Champlain played a major role in this battle by advancing in front of the Algonquins with his bright breastplate armor and his musket. Killing two indians, who turned out to be chiefs, the Iroquois fled, but not before many were killed by the Algonquins. It is recorded that the Iroquois never forgot or forgave the French and, coupled with their hatred of the Algonquins, the French and Iroquois animosity was to endure in various degrees for almost a century afterwards.

It should be noted that this 1609 battle account took place early in the 17th century, before most indians had or were familiar with European firearms. By the later 17th century, Jean and Hilaire's time, many indians had acquired firearms and warfare between the French and the Iroquois had become more lethal to both sides.

The Richelieu River continued to be a militarily strategic waterway route running north and south between the St. Lawrence River and Lake Champlain and Lake George. It was the route used by both the French colonists and the British colonists right up through the French and Indian wars. It continued to be a strategic thoroughfare through the American Revolution when the English, now occupying the former French colony, traveled south to do battle with Washington's American armies.

In 1668, after a three-year tour of duty, the Carignan regiment was returned to France. Because Louis XIV was anxious to increase the size of his small colony, any soldiers who wished to stay in New France were given an opportunity to remain and also get out of the army. Additionally, a grant of free farming land for those who wanted it was an extra incentive. Along with 400 other soldiers, both Jean and Hilaire chose this attractive option and remained in New France.

While they were in the army, it's possible that Jean and Hilaire were stationed in the same area. I suspect, however, that this was not the case. My reason for this suspicion is that after they exited the army in 1668, they settled in different areas. Jean settled across the St. Lawrence River from Montreal in a small town called St. Ours, which was located on the eastern bank of the strategic Richelieu River. Hilaire appears to have settled in the Quebec City area. It is possible these areas were where they had been stationed in the army, therefore, their familiarity made them a first choice for settlement. Of course, this is just conjecture and there could be numerous other possibilities. Rather than go into farming as Jean did, Hilaire may have settled in Quebec City to pursue an urban occupation. Where they were stationed and why they settled where they did cannot be known with certainty.

It must be remembered that Jean and Hilaire are footnotes to history. They lived in an age when military men, volunteer soldiers, were common men who were most often members of the poor lower class. Therefore, we must reconstruct their lives from meager records of the time, which really doesn't tell us much. These were not scholarly or important men who left diaries or who were written about in history books or accumulated titles, fortunes or fame. Being of the Catholic faith their unnoticed lives were solely, and fortunately for history, recorded in the local church records of births, baptisms, marriages and finally deaths and burials.

As the summer of 1668 began and the Carignan regiment departed for its return to France, Jean and Hilaire were again on the threshold of new lives. No longer would they have the security of knowing that the French army would provide their food, lodging and salary. They were now private citizens of a small struggling French colony. They were now thousands of miles from their families and the civilization that had raised them, and were without the benefit of their former surrogate army family.

CHAPTER 3

Jean LeTellier 1668-1704

The Years 1668 to 1688

Upon his separation from the army, Jean settled near a small town called St. Ours, which was located on the eastern bank of the Richelieu River. Because of its strategic location on the north-south waterway between Montreal and British New England, it is probable that there was a French military detachment in the St. Ours area. Such an establishment would have given security to the small town and the local farmers.

As a single man with no family and a new farm to develop, Jean would have struggled to build a dwelling, acquire farm animals and clear and cultivate his land. Church records indicate that he did not marry for another nine years, at which time he was 35 years old. By this time, his farm would have been fairly well established and as a bachelor he would have been considered a respectable catch for a prospective bride.

In this early period of New France's history, wives were a very scarce commodity. Due to this scarcity, French fur trappers often married indian women, but French soldiers and bachelor farmers often had to do without wives. The man-to-woman ratio in the

1670's was approximately ten to one.

Because of this scarcity of women in the predominantly male French colony, Louis XIV instituted a state-sponsored immigration program that sent single young women from France to New France as prospective brides. These women were called "Filles du Roi" (King's Daughters) and approximately 800 women were sent to New France between 1663 and 1673. All expenses for the journey and housing upon arrival were paid for by the French government and the King granted a dowry of from 50 to 100 livres upon marriage.

Upon arrival in New France, the prospective brides were chaperoned and put into dormitory-style lodging until they had selected, and been selected by, prospective husbands. These lodgings were often in Catholic convents in Montreal and Quebec City. The young women were able to choose their husbands and were not forced to marry any particular individual. One can picture newly arrived young women meeting a prospective husband and the couple virtually interviewing and sizing each other up under the watchful eyes of a chaperone who was often a religious nun.

In spite of their contracts with the King, there were cases where women did not choose to marry. Some of these women returned to France and others stayed in New France, sometimes marrying years later. In some cases, women who were themselves not selected by men for marriage chose to remain in the colony as household servants, and subsequently became spinsters.

The Filles du Roi (Filles) were recruited in France by various Catholic parishes and charitable institutions, mainly in the northern cities such as Paris and Rouen. Surely not by coincidence, the largest number of Filles arrived in the three-year period 1669-1671, following the demobilization of Jean and his 400-regimental companions who chose to remain in New France in 1668. There is no proof that Jean married a Fille, and given his nine years of single life after leaving the army, it is possible that when he did marry his wife was not a Fille. This theory is supported by the fact that Louis XIV's program was halted in 1673, which was four years before Jean actually married in 1677. Though the record and brief biographies of individual Filles is substantial, it is not complete, therefore it may never be known whether or not Jean's wife was a Fille du Roi.

Between Jean's settlement in St. Ours and his marriage, we have three notary records that he bought and sold land in the area. These records were notarized on January 19, 1671, May 23, 1673 and May 1, 1676. In each transaction we find Jean signing his name using his characteristic mark.

Being fairly well established by the year 1677, Jean Baptiste LeTellier met and chose to marry one Marie Madeleome Gratot on the 28th of April in Boucherville, Chambly, Quebec. As per church directives, the marriage would have taken place in the morning, and Jean and Marie Madeleine would have taken the sacraments the previous day. Also, as per the established New France custom, the marriage contract would be formally notarized and recorded. It is interesting to note also that the marriage took place after Easter, in keeping with the Catholic Church's directive that no marriages be performed during Lent.

One year after their marriage, a daughter, Marie Anne Tellier (March 7, 1678) was born. Their second child, also a daughter, named Catherine Tellier, was born on March 24, 1680. Their third daughter, named Marie Madeleine Tellier, followed on October 6, 1682. It is interesting to note that the "Le" of the LeTellier surname was apparently dropped by Jean for his children's surnames.

Finally, on October 26, 1687 Marie Madeleine presented Jean with a son, who they appropriately named Jean Baptiste Tellier. One can imagine Jean's joy when, at the respectable age of 45, his first son was born and named after himself.

Tragedy was to very quickly destroy Jean's short-lived joy. The records indicate that Jean's five year old daughter, Marie Madeleine, died on October 29, 1687, three days after his son's birth. The next day, October 30, we get the recorded death of his seven year old daughter, Catherine. On November 1, 1687, Jean's 25 year old wife, Marie Madeleine, died. In a period of three days, Jean had lost two daughters and his wife.

The final tragedy was to follow within less than two months. The day before Christmas, December 24, 1687, Jean's ten week old son, Jean Baptiste Tellier, died.

Given the longevity of modern man, it is difficult for us to comprehend such a tragedy. Since no cause of death is listed in the historical records, one can only speculate as to the cause of the tragedy. Quite possibly it was an epidemic that took away all but one daughter of Jean's family. However, given the proximity of their recorded deaths and the constant indian problems in the early French colony, it could equally have been the result of an indian attack. The reasons are lost to history, and all that we can be certain of is the deep grief and despair that Jean must have experienced.

The Years 1688 to 1690

The constant struggle for survival in a harsh world and the fact that he still had one daughter, nine year old Marie Anne to care for, would have made it necessary for Jean to immediately carry on with his life. The luxury of an extended period of grief, so common in modern society, was not available to the 17th century pioneers.

One year later, on December 1, 1688, Jean married Anne Chenier in Pointe Aux Trembles, Montreal, Quebec. As in his first marriage, we have no definitive evidence that Anne was a Fille du Roi. His place of marriage, however, would indicate that she probably came from the town of Pointe Aux Trembles, which is on the north side of the St. Lawrence River, and a few miles east of the old Montreal of the 1600's. It appears that Jean sold his properties in St. Ours, which is on the south side of the St. Lawrence, and bought a farm in Pointe Aux Trembles. Most of Jean's purchases and sales for the remainder of his life appear to have occurred in the Pointe Aux Trembles area and St. Therese Island, which is in the St. Lawrence River.

Unfortunately, on July 2, 1690 tragedy was to again intrude upon Jean's life when his wife of less than two years, was killed in an Indian and British raid. The historian Frances Parkman describes the event as follows:

> '"Captain John Schuyler (the British commander) was permitted to make a raid into Canada with a band of volunteers. Schuyler left the camp at Wood Creek with twenty-nine whites and a hundred and twenty indians, passed Lake Champlain, descended the Richelieu to Chambly, and fell suddenly on the settlement of La Prairie, whence Frontenac had just withdrawn with his forces. Soldiers and inhabitants were reaping in the wheat-fields. Schuyler and his followers killed or captured twenty-five, including several women. He wished to attack the neighboring fort, but his Indians refused; and after burning houses, barns and hayricks, and killing a great number of cattle, he seated himself with his party at dinner in the adjacent woods, while cannon answered cannon from Chambly, La Prairie, and Montreal, and the whole country was astir. 'We thanked the Governor of Canada,' writes Schuyler, 'for his salute of heavy artillery during our meal.'"

One of the "several women" referred to in Parkman's account was Anne (Chenier) LeTellier, Jean's second wife.

In less than three years Jean was forced to deal with a second personal tragedy. Again our modern perspective on life makes it difficult for us to comprehend how Jean was able to carry on. It certainly was only slight consolation to Jean that at least there were, as yet, no children born of this second marriage. The severity of pioneer life in New France certainly would have conditioned Jean to adversity, and possibly Jean's religious upbringing and surroundings would have made him familiar with the Biblical story of Job. When one considers Jean's story, the comparison with Job is surely a valid one.

The Years 1691 to 1704

Consistent with the strengths already demonstrated by Jean, we find that he married for a third time on July 9, 1691 at Pointe Aux Trembles, Montreal, almost a year to the day after losing his second wife. His new wife's name was Marie Renee Lorion and she was the widow of a French soldier named Jean Delpue, who was killed in the same massacre that had taken Jean's second wife. If ever a marriage was one of convenience, this certainly must have been such a marriage. Given the scarcity of women in New France, widows did not remain single for very long.

All indications are that this was a happy and successful marriage and was not scarred by the tragedies of Jean's two previous marriages. Jean continued to farm land in the Pointe Aux Trembles area and, from notarized land purchases and sales, appears to have profitably dealt in land acquisitions throughout his life. Upon his death we have records that he left land to his children and they, in turn, traded, bought and sold land between each other and other individuals.

Five children, three girls and two boys, were born of Jean's third marriage, and their names and dates of birth are shown as follows:

Marie Therese Tellier, b. 4/6/1692

Genevieve Tellier, b. 1/28/1694 – d. 2/15/1694

Jean Baptiste Tellier, b. 9/26/1696

Marie Tellier, b. 1699

Joseph Tellier, b. 8/30/1700

Of particular significance are Jean's two boys. Jean Baptiste Tellier was Jean's second attempt to name a son after himself. As previously mentioned, his first son with this name died when only two months old. It is a testament to Jean's courage and perseverance that he named his second son after his deceased first son and himself. The other significant son, Joseph Tellier, is of particular interest to this author, in that my maternal family tree comes down from Joseph Tellier. My grandfather's name was also Joseph Tellier and he was the seventh generation son down the family tree from the first Joseph Tellier.

On November 9, 1704, four years and two months after Joseph's birth, Jean Baptiste LeTellier died in Varennes, Quebec. He was 62 years old and by any standards considered, those of the 17th century or those of the present century, he had lived an incredible life. As per the previously mentioned New France customs, two years later Jean's widow, Marie Renee Tellier, married one Jean Tifroy, on March 8, 1706.

On September 1, 1715, Louis XIV, the King who had sent Jean Baptiste LeTellier on his life's adventure to the New World, died at the age of seventy eight. He had been on the throne for seventy two years, the longest reign in Europen history. His final hours were spent accompanied by nobility, family and clergy. It is a final coincidence of history (at least to the Tellier family story) that the King's closet clergy present was a Jesuit Priest, who had been made the King's Confessor in 1709. The priest's name was Michel LeTellier (1643-1719), and he was born the son of a French peasant.

An Epilogue to Chapter 3

If one travels in Canada today, he will not find any obvious indications that Jean LeTellier, the French soldier turned farmer, ever existed. He is just one of thousands of early French pioneers that came to New France, endured hardships, settled the land, built homes, families and lives, and anonymously disappeared into history. Few gained sufficient prominence or fame to have their names appear in history books. Their memory exists, if at all, in the minds of their descendents. In Jean's case, this is literally thousands of descendents who bear the surnames LeTellier, Tellier, LaFortune and other names.

However, if one looks at the Montreal area closely, he will in fact find traces of Jean's existence. The small town of Pointe Aux Trembles, where Jean had his farm, is now the southeastern area of the modern island of Montreal, and is known by the same name. Where the farms were located is today fully built up and populated, and incorporated into greater Montreal. Situated between the southeastern Montreal areas of Ville De Montreal and Pointe Aux Trembles is a street called Rue Tellier. This street (rue) is parallel and just north of Rue Notre Dame, the main east-west road running adjacent to the St. Lawrence River. Ironically, Rue Tellier commences, on its western end, just next to a present day Canadian military base called "Base Militaire de Longue-Pointe." One suspects that Jean, the former French soldier, would enjoy this coincidence.

The modern traveler can find another physical indication of Jean's existence. This site concerns Jean's second and third wives, Anne Chenier and Marie-Renee Lorion, respectively. As earlier indicated, Anne Chenier was killed in a battle with the British and the Indians on the shore of the Riviere des Prairies. Also recalled is the fact that one year after Anne was killed, Jean married Marie-Renee Lorion, the widow of Jean Delpue, the French soldier who was also killed in the same battle. The site of this battle can be found on the northeastern shore of the island of Montreal. It is approximately two kilometers directly north of Pointe Aux Trembles, where the Tellier farms were located. A stone memorial with a bronze plaque marks the site today, and describes and commemorates the tragic event. The memorial can be found near Gouin Boulevard and 128th Ave. Gouin Boulevard is the main east-west road which runs along the shore of the Riviere des Prairies.

CHAPTER 4

The Tellier Family in the Agricultural Age, 1704 to the 1880's

Jean LeTellier's Sons: Jean Baptiste Tellier and Joseph Tellier 1704-1731

At the time of his death in 1704, it appears that most of Jean's land holdings were on Ste. Therese Island, which is in the St. Lawrence River adjacent to the Pointe Aux Trembles area. When his widow, Marie Renee, married Jean Tifroy, Jean and Marie's sons, Jean Baptiste and Joseph, would have gained inheritance rights to Jean's lands. At the time of their mother's remarriage, Jean Baptiste was ten years old and Joseph was six. From records of their activities in latter life, such as marriage dates, land transactions, etc., we get indications that Jean Baptiste and Joseph took quite different paths in life. Jean Baptiste appears to have pursued an adventurous lifestyle, while Joseph appears to have followed a more conservative existence.

In 1721 we find Jean Baptiste signing a contract with an individual to go on a canoe journey to western lands, carrying merchandise and bringing back furs. In 1723 the records show that he sold his inheritance rights to St. Therese Island lands to his sister, Therese Tellier, and her husband, Luc LeTouche. Finally, on July 22, 1747, at the age of 51, we find he married an indian named Marie Josephte Macatemic at Michillimackinac (a French fur trading fort located in present day Mackinaw City, Michigan). Father Pierre Du Jaunay, the Jesuit priest who married them noted the following in the Ste. Anne's church records:

> *July 22, 1747 I received the mutual marriage consent of Jean Baptiste Tellier de la Fortune and of Marie Josephte, a Nepissingue woman baptized this morning, by which marriage were legitimized Antoine, 19 years old; Francois Xavier, 14 years old; Ann, ten years old; Ignace, 6 years old; Joseph, 3 years old, and Marie Josephte, 6 months old, their children.*
>
> P. Du Jaunay   Miss. Of the Society of Jesus

Joseph, by contrast, married one Madeline Louiseau on April 6, 1723 at the age of 23. As previously mentioned, Joseph is the author's direct lineage maternal ancestor, therefore, Madeline is also a direct lineage ancestor. Madeline was 19 years old at their marriage. They proceeded to raise a large family of 12 children between the years 1724 (Joachim Tellier) and 1746 (Marie Monique Tellier) on farmland inherited by Joseph.

The Tellier Family Geneology 1731 to 1884

This author's maternal lineage continues down from Joseph's fifth child, Pierre Rene Tellier, who was born in 1731. Joseph Tellier, Pierre's father, was to die in 1777 at the respectable age of 77.

To simplify my generations, I will use a Biblical format. Pierre Rene Tellier begat (with wife Marie Chevalier) a son, Rene Francois Tellier. He in turn begat (with wife Marie Anne Leroux) a son, Pierre Tellier, who in turn begat (with wife Jeanne Joly), a son, Pierre Joseph Tellier. He in turn begat (with wife Marie Josephte Rondeau) a son, Jean Baptiste Tellier, who in turn begat (with wife Angele Mousseau) a son, Henri Tellier. He in turn begat (with wife

Aurelie Sylvestre) a son named Joseph Tellier.

I believe I should pause here and give the reader some perspective as to where we are in the geneological relationship to the author. Henri Tellier and his wife Aurelie (Sylvestre) are my great-grandfather and great-grandmother. They were married in 1857 in a small town a few miles north of the St. Lawrence River, and east of Montreal, called St. Cuthbert. They were to have a family of eight children, three boys and five girls. In the year 1866 they had a son who they named Joseph. This Joseph Tellier was my grandfather. He, like his numerous siblings, was to work on the family farm until he was 18 years old, at which time he married a local girl named Angelina Durand. The year was 1884 and Angelina, at 23 years old, was five years Joseph's senior. The story of these grandparents will be continued in Chapter 7; however, the remainder of this chapter will deal with some information of the Tellier family up to recent times.

Tellier Family Statistics, 1680-1980

It is not possible, nor within the intended scope of this book, to give more detail on the lives of all the generations just listed. However, it is possible, and appropriate, to give the reader some general facts and statistics compiled by contemporary Tellier family members still residing in Canada.

Using information compiled on 4,526 individual descendents of the original Jean Baptiste LeTellier, the following interesting facts emerge (please note that these individuals scan the years from 1680 to the 1980's):

- The average longevity is 55 years.
- The oldest longevity was 101 years.
- Of 869 marriages surveyed, the oldest at marriage was 73 years old and the youngest was 13 years old. The average age at marriage was 27 years old.
- The oldest during maternity was 46 years old.

- The youngest during maternity was 16 years old. Of great interest here is that this girl was Marie Madeline Gratiot, who was Jean Baptiste LeTellier's first wife.
- The average number of children per family was four, and the highest number of children per family was 17.
- Life expectancy (based on total of available ages at death) was 35 years in 1700, 10 years in 1800, 20 years in 1860, 30 years in 1900, 50 years in 1920, 55 years in 1940, 70 years in 1960, and 75 years in 1980.
- Highest percentage of given names duplications on total of individuals: (1) Joseph; (2) Jean-Baptiste; (3) Pierre; (4) Marie; (5) Marie-Louise; (6) Anonyme.
- Highest percentage of surname duplications on total of individuals: (1) Tellier; (2) LaFortune; (3) Tellier dit LaFortune; (4) Letellier; (5) Forest; (6) LeTellier.
- Highest percentages of occupation duplication on total of individuals: (1) farmer; (2) soldier; (3) doctor; (4) teacher; (5) carpenter; (6) priest.

Some other occupations which naturally had smaller percentages of repeat occupations were shopkeeper, lawyer, chemist, accountant, mason, notary, policeman, salesman, and the list goes on. The family also had some notable occupations which included a Canadian Supreme Court justice, Joseph-Mathias Tellier (1861-1952), and a Canadian Minister of Agriculture, Luc LeTellier (1820-1881).

Statistical Observations

A few observations of the above stated statistics should be noted:
- Regarding the average number of children: as farm families in the 17th and 18th centuries, the families, of necessity, would have been large. The overall average would have

been significantly decreased, however, by the smaller average families of the 20th century. The average is calculated up to the 1980's.
- Regarding life expectancy, the families' life expectancies in the 20th century appears to mirror modern accepted actuarial figures for this period. The wide variance in the earlier years, i.e., 35 years in 1700, 10 years in 1800, would be the result of a small base sample used.
- Regarding the average longevity of 55 years over a 300 year period, this average seems quite high, but it is probably due to the fact that of all the family members surveyed, a high number of them lived in more recent times.
- Regarding most duplication of given names, it is gratifying to this author that the name most given was Joseph, which was my grandfather's given name (as well as my own). It is appropriate also that the close runner up's given name is Jean Baptiste, our original ancestor's name.
- Regarding highest percentage of surname duplications, the name Tellier, my grandfather's last name, seems to have developed in the second generation when our original ancestor's birth records for his children is found to have the name prefix "Le" dropped. It also seems predictable that the second most used surname is "LaFortune" which was our original ancestor's "dit" name.
- Finally, regarding highest occupation duplications, again, it is appropriate that the premier occupation is "farmer" and the second occupation is "soldier." Jean Baptiste LeTellier, a French soldier turned farmer, would have definitely approved of his descendents subsequent choice of occupations.

CHAPTER 5

The Limousin, Beaufort, Brunelle Family, 1668 to 1872

Thus far we have covered the story of my maternal family from the Foundling Father, Jean Baptiste LeTellier, to the marriage of my grandfather, Joseph Tellier, in Canada in 1884. This chapter will recount the story of my paternal geneology from the Founding Father, Hilaire Limousin dit Beaufort, in 1668 in New France, to the Brunelle family in Canada in the 1870's.

We will begin the Brunelle family story with my first New France ancestor, Hilaire Limousin dit Beaufort, after he exited the French army in 1668. As previously mentioned he settled in Quebec City, at which time he took up the trade of tailor. Possibly this had been his occupation in France before he entered the French army. Four years after leaving the army, he married a young girl named Antoinette Lefebvre. Fortunately for history, we do know some facts about Antoinette. Though there is only a strong suspicion that my female maternal ancestor (LeTellier family) was a Fille du Roi, there is historical certainty, through records, that Antoinette was a Filles.

Antoinette was born in Chanu, Normandy, France, about 1653 and was the daughter of Charles Lefebvre and Louise

Prudhomme. She came to New France in 1671 as a Filles, bringing with her goods worth an estimated value of 400 French livres as her personal dowry.

Hilaire Lemousin dit Beaufort and Antoinette Lefevbre were married on November 9, 1671 in Quebec City. As per Antoinette's contract with the French government, she received the King's dowry of 50 livres upon her marriage. Neither Hilaire nor Antoinette were able to sign the marriage contract, drawn up on October 29th by notary Becquet.

Hilaire, who was born in 1633, would have been 38 years old. Antoinette was a young woman of 18. Upon their marriage, the couple first lived in Quebec City. Their first born child was a girl who they baptized Genevieve on October 22, 1672. Sadly, the child died three months later, being buried on January 13, 1673.

Though surely saddened by their loss, the next child they had was also a girl and they named her Genevieve. Between the birth of their first child in 1672 and their last child in 1694, Hilaire and Antoinette had 13 children, 10 girls and 3 boys.

On March 31, 1692 they had their twelfth child, a son, who they named Joseph Limousin dit Beaufort. This son is the author's first paternal side ancestor born in the Americas. Long before Joseph's birth, the family had moved from Quebec City to Champlain, Province of Quebec . Possibly they moved to land Hilaire was entitled to when he left the French army. If he had changed careers from tailor to farmer, numerous children would have been beneficial. Of course, there were only three boys in the family which left a lot of farm work for the remaining nine girls.

Hilaire Limousin dit Beaufort died on May 14, 1708, and was buried two days later at Champlain. He had lived to be 75 years old, no small accomplishment in the 18th century. His wife Antoinette survived him by 17 years, dying on May 21, 1725. She had lived to the age of 72, again no small feat, particularly since she had borne 13 children.

Joseph Limousin dit Beaufort (1692-1763) married Marie-Josephte Dubois (1697-1763) on November 25, 1718. Like his parents before him, Joseph also had a large family, which consisted of 12 children. Fortunately for Joseph and Marie, the sex of their children was evenly divided between six boys and six girls. They named their fourth child Francois Limousin dit Beaufort. Francois is the son that begat the author's family.

As was done with the Tellier family, we will use the Biblical format to proceed down the generations. Francois Limousin dit Beaufort married Jeanne Carpentier dit Bailly on November 13, 1753 in Champlain, Province of Quebec. They in turn begat a son who they named Joseph Brunelle dit Beaufort.

The author must pause here to point out to the reader the significant last name change. The family last name (last name plus dit name) went in this generation from "Limousin dit Beaufort" to "Brunelle dit Beaufort." In essence, the Limousin name was dropped and replaced by the Brunelle name. The exact reason for this is unknown to the author.

We can, however, speculate as to what happened. The French "dit" names, which were originally meant to simplify family identification, had after a few centuries begun to totally confuse the issue. Not only did husbands have dit names, but wives also brought dit names to the marriage. In my research of family names for the period, I find that some families had Brunel and Brunelle for their dit names. What probably happened is that this generation decided to just drop one last name and replace it with a Brunelle surname. The author yields to the reader. Your guess is as good as my own.

If the reader is not totally confused, the next change in last name should push the reader "over the edge". On January 12, 1783 Joseph Brunelle dit Beaufort married a Marguerite Moreau in Contral Faribault, Quebec. They in turn begat a son who comes down to us in records with the name Joseph Brunelle. We see here that the original dit name of Beaufort is now completely dropped and we are left with just a given name and single last name. This Joseph Brunelle is the first Joseph Brunelle in my direct linear ancestry. Great Great Grandfather Joseph Brunelle married Madeleine Lavalle on April 8, 1823 in Berthier, Quebec. They begat a son also named Joseph Brunelle. This Joseph Brunelle (my great grandfather) on October 26, 1852 married Valerie Brissette in St. Marcel, Richelieu, Quebec.

Trusting here that the author has not exhausted the reader's interest or patience, I will proceed with the begetting one more time and simply say that my great grandparents, Joseph and Valerie, had a son in 1872 named Arsene Brunelle, who was my grandfather. Both the author and hopefully the reader can breathe easier now that we are out of the quagmire of family geneology. For my own part, my paternal family history to this point is non-personal and just a listing of names, dates and places. With Grandfather Arsene Brunelle, I feel I have arrived at flesh and blood family and memory.

CHAPTER 6

The Arsene Brunelle Family 1872-1920's

The Brunelle Name in History

William Shakespeare's famous question *"What's in a name?"* comes to mind at this juncture of my family story. I believe it is appropriate that before telling the story of my grandfather, Arsene Brunelle, I should convey to the reader a general history and also the derivation of the Brunelle surname.

Brunelle is a French surname that has a nickname origin. It is derived from the physical characteristics or personal attributes of the first bearers of the name. In this case, the surname is derived from the French word "brun" which translated from the French means "brown," with the affixed ending "el." The nickname of brown would have been applied to a person with brown hair, or someone of dark complexion. In the Middle Ages, hair color was very important in the generation of surnames. It is first recorded as a surname in the 12th century, at which time it was passed into England with the French Norman conquests. There is a record of a Robert Brownell marrying one Alice Mathewe in London in 1571.

There were numerous spelling variations of the name, often

depending on the country in which the name was used. Some common names used in France were Brun, Brunel, Brunelle, Brunet, Bruneau and Bruneleau. There are some fairly famous people with name variations found in countries other than France or England. We find Filippo Brunelleschi (1377-1446), the famous Florence, Italy architect and engineer, becoming one of the pioneers of early Renaissance architecture. We also find families named Brunel being granted coats of arms in such diverse areas as Picardy and even Sweden in the year 1650.

Probably the most famous Brunel family in history belongs to a French-born engineer/inventor named Marc Isambard Brunel (1769-1849) and his son, engineer/inventor Isambard Kingdom Brunel (1806-1859). The senior Brunel was born in Hacqueville, France, became an engineer, and in the midst of the French Revolution was forced to flee to the United States because of his royalist sympathies. Upon arriving in New York City, he obtained the post of chief engineer and proceeded to design and build many buildings including an arsenal and cannon foundry. He also improved the defenses of the channel between Staten Island and Long Island (Brooklyn).

After perfecting a method of making ships' pulleys by mechanical means, rather than by hand, he decided to sail to England to market his invention. He arrived in London in 1799, presented his plans to the government and they promptly accepted his proposal. His machine was installed at the navy dockyards in Portsmouth and was one of the earliest examples of completely mechanized production.

Becoming a prolific inventor, he went on to design many more labor-saving machines including the first tunnel shield which he successfully used to build an aqueous tunnel under the Thames River between the years 1825 and 1842. In 1841 he was knighted for this engineering feat.

As significant as Marc's engineering accomplishments were, his fame was to be eclipsed by his son, Isambard Kingdom Brunel.

As an only son, he aided his father in the building of the Thames Tunnel. He then went on to build many ships' docks throughout England. Becoming involved in the expansion of railroads, he eventually oversaw the design and construction of over 1,000 miles of the English railway system. Expanding his talents to marine design and engineering, he built three of England's most famous ships: the Great Western (1837), the Great Britain (1843), and the Great Eastern (1858). The Great Western was the first steamship to provide regular transatlantic service, the Great Britain was the first large iron hull steamship driven by a propeller, and his crowning glory, the Great Eastern, was the largest ship in the world for 40 years. The Great Eastern also had the distinction of being the ship which laid the first Atlantic cable.

An interesting modern sidelight to the careers of the two Brunel engineers occurred in November 2002. The BBC conducted a poll to determine "Who is the greatest ever Englishmen?". Not unexpectedly, Winston Churchill came in number one. Quite unexpectedly, at least to this author, Isambard Kingdom Brunel came in second. Churchill received 447,423 votes. Brunel received 56,000 less. Princess Diana came in third, followed by Charles Darwin, William Shakespeare, Isaac Newton, Elizabeth I, John Lennon, Horatio Nelson, and finally Oliver Cromwell. One wonders if the many thousands of "Brits" who voted for Brunel were aware that his father was a Frenchman.

Arsene Brunelle

After the American Civil War, the Industrial Revolution in the United States had a profound indirect impact on the lives of French Canadians in the province of Quebec. This impact was caused by the textile industry which had located in the numerous mill towns situated along the rivers of the New England states. The history of one such river, the Blackstone in Rhode Island, is representative of many of these rivers. Additionally, one town along the Blackstone, called Manville, is especially representative and germaine to the Brunelle story.

In 1889 (the same year the Eiffel Tower opened), a 17 year old boy named Arsene Brunelle decided to leave his home in St. Marcel, Richelieu, Quebec and immigrate to Manville, Rhode Island. Arsene chose Manville because an older brother had located there and was working in a textile mill. Another older brother had also preceded Arsene to the United States, however, this brother had immigrated to Fall River, Massachusetts and became a pharmacist.

All over the United States, sons as well as daughters of rural America were migrating to cities and mill towns to improve their fortunes. The French Canadian migration to the United States was for the same reasons, however, there appears to be one additional incentive for the French.

By the late 19th century many French Canadian farm families had been in the Americas for over 200 years. Because of this, tillable acreage for individual sons in a large family had decreased over the years. Also, coming from large families, few options were available to sons who didn't inherit the family farm. Before the Industrial Revolution, the choice was to work for a family member or lease land and struggle to make the farm profitable enough to support a family. With the industrialization of New England, the French in Quebec had another option; emigrate to the United States.

Manville, at the time of Arsene's arrival, was a thriving mill town of perhaps 3,000 inhabitants. It was founded in 1811 by a textile mill owner named Thomas Man. Between 1811 and the Civil War, Manville had a few textile mills on the banks of the Blackstone River which employed mostly English-extraction mill workers. After the war, the work force quickly became largely Roman Catholic French Canadians.

Upon arrival in Manville, Arsene lived with his older brother until he was able to get a job in the mill and save some money. It is probable that his brother got him his job. It was a fine custom of the French Canadians to help find relatives work and to put them up in their homes until the new emigrant could get established. Fortunately for Arsene, there was no shortage of jobs in this period. If anything, there was a shortage of able workers.

Arsene promptly got a job as a textile weaver in the huge Manville Mill. By the time of Arsene's employment, the Manville Mill was well on it's way to becoming the largest mill, under one roof, in America. Virtually all of the working citizens in Manville worked in the mill.

The topography of the Blackstone River Valley was typical of many mill rivers in New England. The mill was initially located on a long island that was situated in the river adjacent to the town of Manville. From this location, the mill was able to draw mechanical power from the river using water wheels. With the advent of steam power, the river power was no longer necessary. However, the mill remained and expanded along the length of the island running parallel to the river shoreline.

A "river road" running along the shore ran from Woonsocket, RI, a larger mill town, through the town of Manville and then continued to the small town of Albion, which also had a mill. Manville was situated on the large hill overlooking the mill and the river. The town was approximately two miles in length by one mile in width, running uphill. Incredibly, by the time of Arsene's arrival in Manville, the mill was almost as long as the length of the town. The mill was initially constructed of local fieldstone material, but the major, and latter, portions of the mill were of red brick and wooden beam construction. It stood four stories high in most areas, had a flat roof and square staircase towers spaced along its length for access to the mill floors. The water between the mill and the shoreline had been made into a barge carrying canal in the mid 19th century but by Arsene's time, the canal was no longer in operation. A substantial cast iron bridge was built over the river at the former canal location to give the hundreds, and then thousands, of workers access to the mill. The Manville housing stock consisted of two and three story wooden rental tenement houses, interspersed with occasional private wood dwellings. By the late 1880's, the Manville Mill also constructed brick company-owned houses which they rented to their workers.

As a 17 year old textile weaver, Arsene would have been assigned a number of looms to operate. The job was a stand-up job and required constant movement of the weaver between the looms. Arsene would certainly not have been among the youngest of the workers. It was not uncommon for children, both boys and girls, to start working in the mills in their early teens, 14 and 15 years old. One must remember that the year 1889 was long before the institution of child labor laws, minimum wages and hours, or workmen's compensation for injuries on the job. The hours were long, typically ten hours a day, over a six-day week. By modern work standards, the work was certainly brutal. After a long hard workday, Arsene would probably have had little energy to walk over the cast iron bridge and up the steep hill to his brother's house.

It appears that Arsene quickly adapted to his new occupation and his new life in Manville. By 1892 he had met a French Canadian girl named Marie Lincourt. Marie's family had emigrated to Newport, Rhode Island in 1891 from Quebec Province. Unfortunately, how they met has not been carried down in the oral history of the family. Marie was born in 1869, making her three years older than Arsene. They were married on May 9, 1892 in the Catholic church of St. James in Manville. Arsene was 20 years old and Marie was 23. The young couple rented an apartment in one of the tenement houses on the Manville hill and proceeded to make a home and raise a family . Their first child was a girl, born in April 1893, and they named her Bertha . Their second child, a son, followed in a little over a year in October 1894. They named him Emile. Their third and fourth children were also sons and they were named Romeo (born August 1896) and Antonio (born February 1899. In seven years of marriage Marie bore four children.

While Arsene was raising his family in these years, he was also advancing in his work at the Manville Mill. Sometime before 1900, he had advanced from his weaving position to a job as a loomfixer. Arsene was an intelligent young man who possessed considerable natural mechanical ability. While he performed and increased his skills as a weaver, he also became knowledgeable in how the loom operated. Not all weavers advanced to the position of loomfixer, and obviously Arsene's supervisor recognized his mechanical skill in repairing and keeping his own looms operating.

The position of loomfixer in the textile industry was considered a higher position than many other positions such as weaver or winder. Not everyone had the aptitude or skill to hold down these jobs, therefore, it was a higher paid position than most other manual positions in the industry.

With his family responsibilities, Arsene certainly could make good use of his salary increases. By 1900, the Brunelles had outgrown the rented apartment on the hill and, with Marie pregnant with their fifth child, Arsene made plans to acquire his own house. He and Marie purchased two large building lots over the crest of the Manville hill on the western outskirts of the town.

On March 7, 1901 Marie gave birth to the Brunelle's fifth child, a boy. He was named Herve Joseph Brunelle, and he is of considerable importance to this story in that he is the author's father. Shortly after buying land, Arsene had contracted to have a house built on one of the lots and by the summer of 1901 they happily moved into their new home.

The new dwelling was a handsome late Victorian style house with nine rooms. It was white, two stories in height, with a high double pitched roof with plenty of attic storage space. The basement was constructed of stacked fieldstone. A porch ran the length of the front of the house and continued to run for half the width of the building. The roof of the porch was supported by milled round columns and the porch railings were supported by turned and milled spindles. The upper portion of the porches contained a profusion of Victorian gingerbread and bracket woodwork. The cornice of the upper portion of the house also had milled wooden brackets and the house's windows had movable green shutters. To use the language of the times, one would describe the house as a very commodious dwelling.

Between 1889 and 1900 Arsene had other interests besides his job and raising a family. Being of a social disposition and a music lover, Arsene decided to join the Manville Brass Band. He chose the clarinet and by 1900 he had become an accomplished clarinet player and a valuable member of the band. He also played with the small orchestra that played for musical performances at the Manville Music Hall. The family has a photo of Arsene as a member of a ten-piece orchestra appearing in a performance of "If I Were King" presented in 1900. Also in family possession is a photo of the full Manville Brass Band of 36 members, including the bandleader, standing in front of the Music Hall around the same period.

Arsene's interest in music also extended to his home life, and all of his children were to learn how to play various musical instruments. The family had a piano in the parlor and throughout their lives in the Brunelle house the children and Arsene were to make beautiful music together. As we will see later in the Brunelle story, the children's musical abilities were to play a significant role in their adult lives.

Sometime after my father's birth in 1901, Arsene was to make a contribution to the continuing advancement in textile technology. The Manville Mill had thousands of looms, weaving cotton six days a week, which required considerable maintenance. One of the common weaving loom problems was the breaking of the cotton thread in the loom operation due to incorrect thread tension. When the thread broke, the loom had to be stopped and the thread retied. Multiplied by thousands of looms, this was a costly operation. There were different devices on looms to adjust thread tension to prevent breaking, but few solved the problem to everyone's satisfaction.

Arsene began to work on a solution to the problem and came up with an idea to solve it. He worked it out on paper and then had a prototype model built. He installed it on a loom in the Manville Mill and it worked extremely well. In order to protect his invention, he had it patented at the U.S. Patent Office and hired a salesman to demonstrate his invention to textile machinery manufacturers. A major loom manufacturer called Crompton & Knowles Loom Works was impressed with Arsene's invention. They were apparently impressed that the "Brunelle Friction Let-off," as it was called, "was suitable to all grades of cloth, compact, easy to adjust and convenient for the weaver". These words are taken from a loom fixing manual published in 1924 called *Cotton Loom Fixing* by John Reynolds. Arsene received royalties for every device installed on looms manufactured, and it was a good source of income for the family for a number of years.

The Brunelles From 1901 to 1916

After my father's birth my grandparents had three more children, two girls and a son. Helen was born in 1904, followed by Eugene in 1905 and the last child, Angeline, in 1907. As was the case in most French Canadian homes at this time, French was spoken at home. The Brunelle children went to the St. James parochial school where they learned to read and write in French. French Canadians of the period considered English as the foreign language and it was so taught in church schools in the U.S. Most teenage children at this time went to work at approximately 15 years of age to help support the large families. The Brunelle children, including my father, also went to work in their teens. The youngest son, Eugene, was permitted to go through high school and into a technical school before going to work. The fact that Eugene received more formal education than the older boys was due to the increased affluence of the family by the 1920's. Grandfather Arsene's significant mechanical and musical skills certainly demonstrated he was a Renaissance Man and we can be sure that he had an enlightened awareness of the value of an education.

From stories my father told me and from my own visits to my grandmother's house, I am able to reconstruct what his life was like growing up in Manville and the Brunelle household. The Brunelle home was literally the last house on the edge of town. A large lawn was on the side of the house with only a small lawn in the front. Beyond the side lawn was a forested, small, but steep hill. Beyond the crest of the hill was a great expanse of open fields which led to a beautiful pond. My dad tells me that as boys he and his brothers spent much of their time in the fields and at this pond. They would catch frogs, go fishing and swim in the pond during the summer vacations. Weather permitting, they also went there when they got out of school. In wintertime, they all went skating on the pond (including the girls) and went sleigh riding on the adjacent hill. Of course living in a large family, each of them had chores to perform. This was especially true of the three girls who helped their mother around the house.

Directly across the road from the house was the second lot of land that my grandfather had purchased. This large lot was used for the family vegetable garden. The garden was Grandmother's project throughout her long life. She loved to garden. Of course, when the children were living at home, the great abundance of vegetables it yielded (corn, potatoes, carrots, rhubarb, etc.) contributed to feeding the large family. Grandmother had a huge pressure cooker which she used for canning vegetables for the winter.

In the early 1920's, Romeo Brunelle had built a large chicken coop at the end of the side yard near the base of the hill. It was a long, flat-roofed one story structure which accommodated many chickens. In addition to producing eggs for the family, Romeo sold eggs as an additional source of income.

A property not far from the house was occupied by a commercial dairy. The children did not have to walk far in order to get bottled milk. Commercial delivery was not necessary.

One can see by the above description that life in the Brunelle home was similar to life on a farm, except that it had the advantages of town social life and also Grandfather worked in the town's Manville Mill. My dad told me that he enjoyed his life as a youngster and when I think about it, his life almost sounds like something out of Mark Twain's Tom Sawyer and Huckleberry Finn.

In the evening the children practiced and played their music. Emile and Helen played the piano and organ. Romeo played the trumpet and Antonio played the trombone. My father, as well as a couple of other children, took violin lessons, however, they did not play the instrument in later life. Emile was to become a church organist as an adult and Helen was to enjoy playing the piano throughout her long life (she lived to 89 years). Antonio was to play the trombone in a dance band well into midlife to supplement his regular income.

World War I

One of the Brunelle family portraits handed down to my family is a studio photo taken in 1916. It is a formal portrait typical of the times with all of the family well dressed and in a formal pose. Grandfather Arsene is seated on the left with grandmother Marie seated on the right. The younger children Angeline (standing) and Eugene (seated) are between Arsene and Marie. The rest of the children are standing in the second row.

When this photo was taken, none of the children were yet married and all were still living at home. I don't know if the photo was made for a particular family occasion but I suspect that

Grandfather, who was always well-informed, was concerned that the World War in Europe would involve the United States and his oldest sons. The children's ages when this photo was taken would have been as follows: Bertha 23, Emile 22, Romeo 20, Antonio 17, my father Herve 15, Helen 12, Eugene 11, and Angeline 9. Within the next year Arsene's two oldest sons, Emile and Romeo, would be in the U.S. Army.

When the United States entered the Great War, it was sadly ill prepared. We had few airplanes, virtually no tanks, not enough small arms to provide all the soldiers, and no military logistical system. Soldiers' uniforms were of poor quality and of few sizes. When a soldier went through the supply issuance of a uniform, little or no consideration was given to fit. You took what was handed to you. A photo of Romeo Brunelle during or shortly after basic training shows a handsome young man in baggy fitting army trousers and shirt, ankle to knee leggings and the felt brim campaign hat of the World War I period. I have never seen a photo of my other uncle, Emile, in uniform but he may well have looked the same.

By 1919 the United States had established basic training camps in a number of states from South Carolina to New York and Massachusetts. Coming from Rhode Island, Romeo and Emile probably received basic training in Massachusetts. What position or job a soldier was to perform (i.e. infantry, engineer, service units, etc.) was traditionally made shortly before the soldier left basic training. This is when the Brunelle brothers' talents as musicians was to serve them well. Uncle Emile was assigned to a "Special Services" unit and stationed at Camp Upon on Long Island, New York. As an accomplished pianist , he participated in camp shows and other entertainment that was put on for the boys; USO-type shows if you will. A famous show business song writer by the name of Irving Berlin was also involved in Camp Upton shows while Emile was there.

Uncle Romeo, being accomplished on the trumpet, was nominally made a Company bugler. At some point his talents were fully recognized and he became a member of the 25th Company of the Army Band. A photo of Emile in his band uniform is in stark contrast to his photo, previously described, in his rough, ill-fitting first uniform. He is photographed, holding his trumpet, in a beautifully tailored uniform with a high collar, dress jacket with brass buttons, gold trim around the sleeves, gold striped pants and brimmed hat with a gold band above the brim – a totally handsome picture.

By the spring and summer of 1918, the American army had become fully committed to combat in France. Between the arrival of the first U.S. Division in France in the summer of 1917 and the early spring of 1918, the U.S. troops had been mostly receiving trench warfare training by the experienced English and French. General John J. Pershing, the Commander of the American Expeditionary Force, had wisely insisted that the Americans fight as American units (regiments, divisions, armies, etc.) rather than become integrated with French or British units. Heavy fighting in the American sectors developed early in the summer of 1918 and the American casualties now became significant. Probably for this reason Romeo was, in early fall 1918, put into a combat unit as a bugler and sent to New York City for troopship deployment to France. As Romeo recounts the story, he was on board ship entering the Atlantic Ocean on November 11, 1918. On receiving word that the Armistice was signed that day, the troopship turned around and returned to New York.

Good fortune was to also smile on Uncle Emile. He served out his army tour as a piano player in Special Services. Upon their discharges from the army, they both returned to their previous lives in the Brunelle home in Manville, Rhode Island.

The Post War Period, 1920-1930

As it was for the rest of the country, the early 1920's were relatively prosperous times for the Brunelle family. Those grown children who were still living at home were gainfully employed and contributing income to the Manville household. Grandfather Arsene was still working in the Manville Mill and also receiving royalty monies from his "Brunelle Let-Off" invention.

In this post World War I period, the automobile that was putting the average American on the road was Henry Ford's "Model T". Grandfather Arsene, however, had other ideas. Always first to recognize new technology, he had his eye on something different in the way of personal transportation. In 1922, Walter P. Chrysler was the chairman of the Maxwell Motor Corporation. After Maxwell went out of business in 1923, Chrysler decided to design a new automobile and start his own company. Assembling an experienced auto engineering team, Chrysler designed a totally new auto which was very advanced for its time. The first production automobile with Chrysler's name on it came out in January 1924. It had a six cylinder, 68 horsepower engine, four wheel hydraulic brakes (most autos of the period had only two wheel brakes), and cool large round headlights. It was a four door, soft-top touring car and Arsene managed to become the first Manville resident to purchase one.

The stories about this car are numerous and legendary in the Brunelle family lore. Next to Grandmother Marie, the Chrysler was Grandfather's "love of his life". He had a large two-car garage built in the rear of the house so that his baby would not have to sit out in the cruel New England winters. The other half of the garage was subsequently filled with Uncle Romeo's Packard automobile. The older boys in the family competed with each other to borrow Grandfather's car. Family photos of the time show Grandfather driving his car in parades and sitting in the front of the Brunelle home with grandchildren sitting on the fenders in the late 1920's and early 1930's.

Grandfather also acquired other new technologies of the 1920's. Along with an earlier console hand cranked Edison record player, one found the newest crystal and radio sets sitting in the parlor. In modern language, one might say Grandfather was a "gadget nut".

Between 1920 and 1929 all except one of the Brunelle children were to marry and move out of the Manville home. Aunt Helen did not marry until sometime in the 1930's. My father Herve Brunelle was to marry in 1924. His story, and my mother's, will be told in Chapter V8.

CHAPTER 7

The Joseph Tellier Family 1884-1923

Family Life In Canada 1884-1903

In the previous chapter we covered the story of my paternal grandparents, the Arsene Brunelles, from Arsene's immigration to the United States in 1889, to the family in the 1920's. This chapter will return to my maternal grandparents, the Joseph Telliers, and pick up where we left them in Chapter Four.

As previously told, Joseph Tellier married Angelina Durand in the small town of St. Cuthbert, Province of Quebec in the year 1884. Joseph was eighteen years old and Angelina was twenty three. They were married in the beautiful Catholic church of St. Cuthbert which was built between the years 1879 and 1884. The exterior of the edifice is constructed of large rectangular cut gray stones which may have been quarried in the province of Quebec. The front entrance consists of a large wooden central door with two matching side doors. The facade is completely symetrical and two large white pointed wooden spires cap the stone main structure of the church. Upon entry, one is confronted by a light and delicate French Baroque interior. Square, beautifully decorated columns flank the pews of the main aisle. The expansive overhead half round ceiling consists of light blue panels with gold medallions in their centers. The beige color of the columns is carried up and around the ceiling, acting as a separation for the blue ceiling panels. All of the painted detailing throughout the church is gold leafed. Three hugh brass chandliers with numerous glass globed lamps are suspended from the high ceiling. Although the town was, and is today, a small farming community, it's church is a testament to the old French tradition of building and supporting grand churches. Grandmother Angelina must have made an impressive entrance down the central aisle of such a church. She was a new bride taking her marriage vows in a new church.

The above description of the church is a contemporary one based on a visit the author made to St. Cuthbert in September 2001. The description of the town and it's surrounding area that follows is also based on that visit. One imagines that probably not much has changed in St. Cuthbert since 1884. While driving to the town, one notices that the topography of the area is a flat, fairly treeless farmland. Fields are predominantly planted with "cow corn" and one is not aware that the town is near until the twin white spires of the church appear, as if growing out of the cornstalks. One turns from the main, two lane, road into what becomes the main and apparently only street of the town. Passing no more than a dozen neatly kept old houses, one comes upon the Catholic Church on the right and a convent house across the street from the church. The three story mansard roofed convent, built in 1882, is constructed of stone similar to the church and has an attached three story red brick structure with a victorian gingerbread porch. A greystone two story building to the right of the convent served as the parochial school (academy) for the parish.

Approximately fifty feet to the right of the church stands a French style parish house constructed in 1876. It is a handsome stone structure of three stories with a steep sloped roof, windowed dormers and an ornate victorian porch around the front and side of the second floor. A wide staircase leads up to the main entrance on the front porch. In it's prime, this Parish House would have comfortably accomodated several priests. Today a single priest serves the entire parish and one suspects he often feels quite alone in such a large house.

The former convent building is now a home for the elderly and the former school building appears to be used for some municipal purpose. Directly to the left of the church is an old, stone enclosed cemetary whose rear and side walls are still surrounded by open farm fields. If one continues on the main street out the other end of town, no more than two or three dozen houses are encountered. They also are old, well maintained French style homes. Most are of two stories with natural stone ends and wooden front and rear facades. Stone chimneys occupy one stone side of the house. The roofs are steep and often gambrel in style with protruding windowed dormers. The only exterior concessions to modern progress appears to be that many of the wooden facades are clad in aluminum or vinyl siding. Traveling out of town one encounters a neat but totally unmodified French Style farmhouse surrounded by a rail style fence. This farm-house appears to retain all of the characteristics and charm of centuries past and is probably fairly representative of the house in which Joseph and Angelina, and all my forebearers, raised their families.

As with all my ancestors, my Tellier grandparents had a large family. Between 1884 and 1903 they had nine children; three boys and six girls. The oldest was a son who they named Napoleon. The youngest was a daughter who they named Marie Antoinette. This daughter, born June 4, 1903, is my mother. In her early years she was to adopt the first name of Alice and kept the Antoinette as a middle name, using the initial A. From a historical perspective, it's interesting to note that seven months after Mother's birth, the Wright Brothers made the world's first successful powered flight (December 17, 1903). The other children, in order of birth after Napoleon, are: Annette (b1888), Philbert (b1889), Marie Ann (b1891), Marie Louise (b1893), Alphonse (b1896), Diana (b1899), Marie Rose (b1901), and my mother in 1903. A son named Joseph Romeo was born in 1905 and died in 1906.

Grandfather's two oldest sons, Napoleon and Philbert, would have been of great help to him on the farm but as we will see, future events made the assistance of the younger children less significant in this area. Raising a large family on a small rented farm in the late 19th century was a constant struggle. As mentioned in the previous chapter, diminishing farm acreage per family had become a real problem. All of the Tellier family descendants were certainly facing these same economic problems that grandfather Joseph was facing. Some Tellier families, along with other French farm families, moved westward to the Manitoba Province of Canada. Just as in the United States where immigrants from Europe were settling the western farm lands of Iowa, Kansas, Nebraska, etc., French Canadians were moving west in Canada.

The Red River Valley area of Manitoba offered plentiful and desirable agricultural land to the hard pressed French farmers in Quebec Province. It offered an opportunity to establish larger farms which could be of greater commercial value. In the 1880's, many French Canadians migrated to the west and formed their own French communities and towns, many with French names. Not co-incidentally, the Canadian Minister of Agriculture between 1873 and 1876 was Luc Letellier. He was aware of the farmers' problems and recognized the agricultural potential of Manitoba. His agricultural policies helped to settle these western lands and there is a town named "Letellier" in the French area of Manitoba.

Apparently grandfather Joseph chose not to exercise the western option. In 1898 he made a brief exploratory visit to the United States, staying with family in Rhode Island. Returning to the farm in St. Cuthbert, he and Grandmother Angelina had three more daughters: Diana (1899), Marie Rose (1901) and Mother in 1903. After my mother's birth, Grandfather and Grandmother made the final decision to immigrate to Woonsocket, Rhode Island. In essence, they chose not to remain in the Agricultural

Age in Canada, but rather they chose to enter the Industrial Age in New England. They chose Woonsocket because it was a large textile center with an abundance of mill jobs and also because Grandmother had family (Durands) who had already located there.

In 1904, with my mother just a year old, and about ready to walk, the entire Joseph Tellier family, six girls and three boys, boarded a train which took them to Rhode Island, U.S.A. My mother tells me that her older sister said that when Mother got extremely restless, Grandmother enlisted the help of the older children to amuse Mother, as well as aunt Marie Rose, who was two years old, and Diana who was four. Throughout Mother's growing years this was the drill; the older children helped with the younger. One tends to forget that the age difference between Mother and her oldest brother, Napoleon, was seventeen years. In any case, the train journey to New England must have been a long arduous trip for the entire family.

When I do the math, I realize that grandmother Angelina was forty-two years old when Mother was born. After having had eight previous children (actually nine, since one died in childbirth), she must have been exhausted by Mother's time. One can be fairly certain that the preparation for the move to the U.S.A. and the actual move surely took its toll on Grandmother.

Grandmother Angelina had a brother living in the Social District of Woonsocket and he and his family kindly agreed to 'put up' the entire Tellier family until jobs and a place to live could be found. As mentioned in relation to grandfather Arsene Brunelle who first went to live with his brother in Manville, it was an old French tradition to help family members get settled in the new country. Surely though, brother Durand was a saintly man to accommodate his sister's eleven member family. Grandfather Joseph was to provide the same hospitality to other family members looking to relocate in the United States.

Grandfather found a job as a teamster delivering raw cotton

and wool bales from the Woonsocket railroad station to the numerous textile mills. Having been a farmer all his life, he was well acquainted and experienced with horses and I suspect he much preferred this work to being enclosed in a mill operating a textile machine. The three oldest children were to easily find mill jobs and the remaining children were registered at St Ann's parochial school in the Social District. Of course, Mother, Aunt Marie Rose, and Aunt Diana were at this time still too young to attend school.

It is appropriate at this point in the Tellier story to give the reader a brief description of grandfather Joseph. He was clearly a man who could easily handle a team of horses. He was a big man for the times, certainly for a Frenchman. He was an inch short of six feet tall with a strong build, large hands, light colored hair and blue eyes. I derived the possible description of my first maternal ancestor in the Americas (Jean Baptiste LeTellier), found in Chapter One, from the above description of grandfather Joseph Tellier. Most probably the Nordic characteristics of my ancestors came from their Normandy roots and the Viking invaders of that area.

Family Life in the United States 1904-1907

If the name Woonsocket now sounds famaliar to the reader, it may be because I also mentioned it 'in passing' in my description of the town of Manville, where grandfather Brunelle settled. Woonsocket is just a half dozen miles up the Blackstone River from Manville and like Manville became a textile manufacturing center in the Blackstone Valley of Rhode Island. Woonsocket is a 'catchy' sounding name which is Indian in origin. One theory is that it's derivation is from two indian words: "woone" which means "thunder",and "sukete", meaning mist. These would have been references to the Woonsocket Falls on the Blackstone River. The earliest white settlers in the area built a sawmill in the 1660's which was powered by the river below the Woonsocket Falls. In the early 18th Century, Quakers settled in the area as well as other farming families. What really started the entire Blackstone Valley on it's Industrial Revolution period occurred in the 1790's when Samuel Slater built the first successful textile mill in the United States on the Blackstone River. This mill still stands in the town of Pawtucket, Rhode Island.

Woonsocket received it's first textile mill in 1810 called the Social Manufacturing Company. By the 1880's, six closely spaced mill villages had developed along the Blackstone River in the Woonsocket area. In the year 1888 these villages were incorporated into the City of Woonsocket, and the individual villages kept their names and identities as separate districts of the city. The Social District was the area where my grandparents settled and was the predominant French Canadian district of the city. At the time of it's incorporation Woonsocket had a population of 20,000 people and 8,000 of these identified themselves as French Canadians. By 1895 Woonsocket had a population of 25,000 and the French Canadians had gained sufficient political power to elect Aram Pothier as the city's first French Canadian mayor. By 1906 a state census indicated that 44 percent of the voters in Woonsocket were of French Canadian ancestry. After two terms as mayor, Pothier subsequently went on to become a seven term governor of Rhode Island. A few miles north in Massachusetts, similar political gains were being made by the Irish, culminating in the election of James M. Curley, the Irish mayor of Boston. He also went on to become a state governor (a four term governor of Massachusets).

By coincidence, the political emergence of Mayor Curley was fictionally documented by the novel "The Last Hurrah". The author of this book is Edwin O'Connor who was born and raised in Woonsocket.

The Social District in which the Tellier's settled was almost 100 percent French Canadian. One did not need to speak English to get along in this area. All of the commercial businesses (food stores, pharmacies, hardware stores, etc.) owned by French Canadians or other proprietors, of necessity spoke French. The Sunday masses in the Catholic Church were in French and the parochial schools used French as the primary language. One did not require a knowledge of English to get a mill job and in fact most French Canadians were employed in the textile mills. As mentioned in reference to the Brunelle family, most large French Canadian families were, by force of economic circumstances, compelled to send their children to work in their mid teens. A 1907 Rhode Island state inspection found that of 8,099 mill hands in Woonsocket, 704 were children between the ages of 14 and 16.

The main housing stock in the Social District consisted of three and four story tenement houses. These were wood structures with large open porches on each floor. The apartments were very basic "cold water flats". Lighting in 1904 was furnished by ceiling and wall gas light fixtures and one paid his lighting bill to the Woonsocket Gas Works. Heating and cooking was accomplished on coal, gas or kerosene fired stoves. The largest room in the apartment was usually the combined kitchen/dining/living room area. Of course there were no electrical appliances, therefore, all clothes washing was done by hand, usually in cold water. Over the years of my mother's childhood, the Telliers moved to a number of these "cold water flats", all within the Social District. Running an eleven member household must have been an extremely tiring job for grandmother Angelina. Additionally, Grandfather's mother, Great Grandmother Aurelie Sylvestre Tellier had come to Woonsocket to live with the family. Grandmother Angelina's health began to seriously deteriorate in this period. She had developed a bronchial illness whose symptoms resembled, but was not , comsumption (or tuberculosis as we know it today).The Tellier family was to later become more knowledgeable about this bronchial condition since many of Angelina's children were to eventually succumb to the illness in later life.

Despite this illness, my grandparents were to have one more

child after my mother. He was born in May 1905 just a year after the family arrived in Woonsocket. He was baptized Joseph Romeo Octavien Tellier. He lived but eighteen months and died on November 5th, 1906. Although infant mortality was much higher a hundred years ago, it is probable that Joseph was born a sickly child, considering Angelina's ill health. (The cause of death was listed as "whooping cough".)

My mother's earliest recollection of Grandmother Angelina is that in the afternoons my mother would lie down with her mother to take a nap. This rest period was surely for Grandmother's benefit as well as Mother'. One also suspects that Grandmother, knowning that the end was near for herself, wished to hold her soon-to-be motherless youngest child close to her.

On November 10, 1907, almost a year to the day after Joseph's death, Grandmother Angelina died. She was forty six years old. Mother was only three and a half years old. Incredibly, despite her young age, another of Mother's early recollections is that Grandmother was wearing a purple dress in her casket. I suspect that the shock to a young child of seeing her dead mother contributed to Mother's vivid recollection over the years. Grandmother was buried in the same grave as her son Joseph and a tombstone with both their names was erected. Of course the inscriptions were in French.

At this point in the story of Joseph Tellier's family, I am acutely conscious of the strong similarity between Grandfather Joseph's loss and our first ancestor's loss two hundred and twenty years before. One recalls that Jean Baptiste LeTellier lost his first wife and three children in a few month's period in 1687. I seriously doubt if Grandfather knew the story of our first ancestor in the Americas but surely the feeling of grief was no less for Grandfather than it was for Jean Baptiste. Also, an additional similarity to their tragedies is noted when one considers that both lost sons were named after their fathers (Jean Baptiste and Joseph).

Not suprisingly, and possibly due to some inherent strength

in the gene make-up of the Tellier family, Grandfather, like Jean Baptiste, quickly carried on with life. All of Grandfather's nine children were still living at home and the youngest, Mother, had yet to begin school. Being five years younger than Grandmother, Grandfather would have been just forty-one years old.

Mother tells me that the first thing Grandfather did within the week of Grandmother's funeral was to march the entire family down to the local photographic studio. As fate would have it, no photograph of the entire family had ever been taken. Grandfather must have keenly regretted this failure and was determined to immediately remedy the situation while the entire family was still living at home. Consequently, the first and only complete Joseph Tellier family photograph that has come down to my own generation was with certainty taken a few days after November 10, 1907.

In this photograph Grandfather is seated to the extreme left in the front row and Mother's oldest sister, Annette, is seated to the extreme right. Mother is seated on a high stool next to Grandfather and she is wearing a white dress, a large white bow in her hair and two waist length curls falling down from her shoulders. Seated on a chair next to Mother is my Aunt Marie Rose who would have been six years old at the time. The other six children are standing in the second row with the two youngest , Alphonse (11 years old), and Diana (8 years old), standing in the middle. Grandfather and all of the children, except Mother, are dressed in either black or navy blue. Grandfather and Uncle Napoleon have small religious crosses (probably from the funeral) in their lapels. To the casual observer, one might mistake Aunt Annette as the mother of the family since she looks very mature in the photography. Grandfather and all the boys are wearing suits with ties and Alphonse is sporting a smart black bow tie; a handsome photograph especially if one doesn't know the history of why it was taken. In many respects it is very similar to the Brunelle family photograph previously described.

Alice Tellier: Early School Years 1908-1912

Marie Antoinette (Alice) Tellier turned five years old in June 1908 and was registered to begin school in September. As were most Catholic children in the Social District , she was enrolled in the local St. Ann's School which had opened in 1903. This school was actually a chapel-school since the main St. Ann's Church had not yet been built (it was to be completed in 1918). The building was a three story brick structure topped by a wooden fourth story mansard style roof with windows. The church portion had a 1,000 seat capacity auditorium and the school section had a large assembly room and twelve classrooms. The teaching nuns were Sisters of the Presentation of Mary and the school had approximately 700 pupils. The children also had the use of a fine gymnasium building which was built in 1894. It contained up-to-date gym equipment, an indoor circular track, two bowling lanes and a billiard room.

For the next nine years Mother's life, both scholasticly and socially, was centered around St. Ann's. Though the class sizes were large, the Sisters were dedicated to their religious calling and the teaching profession. In addition to the traditional reading, writing and arithmethic, Mother also received the religious training common to all Catholic schools. All subjects were taught in French and any instruction given in English was handled as if English was the foreign language. It was not uncommon in these years for children to leave St. Ann's with little or no knowledge of English. (In later years, the 1920's and 1930's, French was taught specifically in the mornings and English was used in the afternoons.) In most cases when children returned home, only French was spoken.

Of course children in Woonsocket who attended public schools were taught in English. Also, any Catholic children who attended the predominantly Irish-Catholic Sacred Heart Parish School were taught only in English. The Church of the Sacred Heart predated St. Ann's Church and was located in the Irish Fairmont

District of Woonsocket. The tradition of ethnic parochial schools and churches was to continue well into the 1970's and 1980's in Woonsocket. Although the French became the dominant ethnic group, after 1900 groups of Polish, Italians, Ukrainians and Romanians also immigrated to the city. Many of these peoples also formed their own parishes and schools.

Although Mother received the abbreviated education common to the times, it apparently was a good basic education. Even in old age, her writing, reading, and mathematics skills were more than adequate. Of course her English, both verbal and written, did not fully develop until after she was sixteen years old but this is getting ahead of the story.

Much of French Canadian life was centered around the Catholic Church and the home. A good amount of Mother's religious and social life was through her involvement with the church sponsored young girls group called "The Angels of Mary" (Les Anges de Marie). In the summertime, the girls would go on picnics and swimming outings at local lakes. Some of the earliest family photographs of Mother show her at such events. She is found in group pictures of girls in white cotton skirts and blouses all wearing identical white summer hats. In one photograph, Mother is standing next to a priest and two other teen age girls. They are standing in front of a hard wheeled pre World War 1 bus. Incredibly, when I showed the picture to Mother a few years ago, she identified the priest as Father Demaras. Quite a memory.

Just as Cub Scouts graduate to become Boy Scouts when they
get older, when the girls got to their teen years, the society was called "The Children of Mary" (Les Enfants de Marie). One picture shows Mother and friends in vintage bathing suits and another shows them apparently dressed for a theatrical performance. Just as my father told me that he enjoyed his childhood years, Mother also said that she enjoyed life when she was a young girl.

Sometime around 1908 or 1909, Mother's grandmother

Aurelie died. Mother doesn't remember much about her grandmother except that she was a heavy woman who was usually found sitting in a rocking chair. By this time, most of Mother's aunts and uncles on both sides of the family (Telliers and Durands) had settled in Rhode Island. In addition to her siblings, Mother had many cousins living in the Social District with which to associate.

Mother only went back to visit Canada on one occasion as a child when she was about eight years old. She recalls staying in a large home which belonged to one of her father's relatives who was a doctor. She returned to Canada a second time in 1967 when she, my father and myself went to visit the World's Fair in Montreal.

Despite the loss of her mother at an early age, Mother was well cared for and had a happy home life. Though Grandfather was a no-nonsense man, he was also a kind and fair man. The children were well informed as to how Grandfather expected them to behave. Mother says that the child raising advice he gave her upon her own marriage was: When you give directions to your children, see that they are followed. In this way they know that "you mean business" and will respect you. I think, however, that Grandfather's most important advice to his children remained unspoken. It was the example he set by how he lived his own life. It's a strange coincidence to me that Theodore Roosevelt, who was president of the United States in 1903 when Mother was born, said it best in one of his talks. In a speech given to the Oyster Bay, N.Y. Holy Name Society on August 16, 1903 he stated "It is no use to preach to children if you do not act decently yourself.". French Canadians valued the family and the home, and considering it's size, the Tellier family was a harmonious and loving family.

A Loss of Home: 1913-1917

By the time Mother was ten years old (1913), four of the Tellier children had married, leaving Mother, three sisters and a brother still living at home. Aunt Annette had married a farmer named Etienne Lebel in 1908 and a year later they had their first child, Marguerite. Uncles Napoleon and Philbert had both married in 1910 and by the next year they also had children, Albert and Fleurette, respectively. Napoleon had returned to farming and eventually purchased a dairy farm (with some financial assistance from his as yet unmarried brother Alphonse) in Cumberland, Rhode Island. Uncle Philbert continued working in a Woonsocket textile mill. Aunt Marie Louise had married a Carpenter's Union treasurer and their first child, Gerald, was born in 1918. Actually, by 1913 Grandfather already had six grandchildren. All of the families just mentioned had large families and by 1937, when Grandfather's last grandchild was born, the final count was 53 grandchildren. To state it more analytically, over a 28 year period of the early 20th Century, grandfather's nine children had, on the average, exactly 1.89 children per year. A prolific family by any standards and as we will see later in the story, the Telliers made a significant contribution to America's World War II effort.

Sometime in this period (1913), Grandmother Angelina's sister introduced Grandfather to a widow, who was a member of the Durand family. She had five children, two boys and three girls, and she lived in her own house in Woonsocket. In keeping with the time honored French tradition of widowers marrying again, Grandfather remarried.

Having married at the young age of eighteen the first time, it is fairly certain that Grandfather felt the need for companionship after Grandmother died. Added to this need was the new imperative of raising the five remaining younger children without the assistance of his now married older children. Considering that his new wife's circumstances were similar to his own, the marriage may have been as much for mutual convience as for companionship. In any case, after they married, Mother's family gave up the Social District flat and moved into their stepmother's house.

The next few years turned out to be a very dark period in

Mother's life. It was equally difficult times for Aunts Marie Louise, Diana, Marie Rose, Uncle Alphonse and ultimately Grandfather Joseph. Unlike the fictional American TV sitcom of the 1970's, The Brady Bunch, where two families come together in harmony and bliss, the attempt to marry a widow and widower and their families was a complete disaster.

It is difficult to look back over nine decades and determine what happened. Apparently the experience for Mother and her siblings was so bad that the entire chapter was never discussed by the Tellier family in later years. My cousin Rene Tellier says that many of the cousins were not even aware that Grandfather had married a second time. Rene relates that his father, Uncle Alphonse never brought the subject up and it wasn't until he and his brothers and sisters were older that they found out. Even then the subject was discussed in hushed tones by his parents.

Mother was not quite as secretive about the story. From her accounts, it appears that all the Tellier children were badly treated in their stepmother's house. The old "wicked stepmother" fable was reality for the years Mother and her siblings spent there. Mother's oldest stepbrother was especially offensive. In addition to constantly taunting Mother, he was a kleptomaniac who stole money and personal possessions from the family. He literally stole anything that wasn't "nailed down". According to Mother, one of the items he stole was Aunt Marie Rose's skates. The family was eventually forced into living in a defensive manner at home.

It is to Mother's credit that she did not lose her sense of humor under these conditions. She related to me the story of her stepmother's washing machine which occurred around the year 1917. It appears that the machine broke down and her stepmother called in the repairman. After the repairman had examined the machine he announced with amazement "Lady, this machine doesn't have a motor.". It seems that Mother's stepbrother had removed the motor and sold it.

Life was made unpleasant in other ways for the Tellier children.

Though the Tellier family was never well off, food had always been plentiful at home. Grandfather always saw to it that the family ate well. For him this was a priority. Under their stepmother's management, food was always in short supply and the children were convinced she was depriving the Tellier children of food.

Finally, there was the question of Grandfather's "savings". Though Grandfather did not scrimp on important things, the Tellier family generally lived frugally. They lacked many comforts we now take for granted such as carpets and floor coverings. The cold water flats that they had lived in provided bare essential living. Because of this frugality, Grandfather was able to save money in three separate savings accounts. It was probably put in three accounts to distribute the loss risks. We must remember this was long before the establishment of the Federal Deposit Insurance Corporation of the New Deal era. Also, this was the pre-Social Security years and one had to plan and provide for one's own retirement. Grandfather mistakenly trusted and relied on his new wife's management of his salary and the savings he brought to the marriage. Sometime within the early years of their marriage, two of the three savings accounts were completely emptied by Grandfather's wife and mysteriously her house mortgage was completely paid off. So much for Grandfather's retirement funds.

Despite the deprevations of life in her new surroundings, Mother's life pretty much continued on it's previous routine. She continued to attend St. Ann's school and participate in it's attendant social life until she reached the age of 14 (1917). She was then abruptly transferred to the local public school. Mother does not know why this occurred but I suspect that her stepmother convinced Grandfather that there were less costs associated with sending the children to public school. Although Grandfather was not an educated man, he had always given his children's education the highest priority and had held his children in parochial school as long as possible. The economy regarding Mother was most assuredly her stepmother's idea. A few months after entering public school, Mother left school forever and began her work career. This was all the formal schooling she would ever receive.

The End of Childhood: 1917-1923

Mother tells me that her first job upon leaving school was with the French Worsted Company, a French-owned textile mill which opened in Woonsocket in 1906. Being a young girl with no work experience, she was given the very menial job of sweeping up the floors between the textile machines. She did this for a short while and then was assigned a job packing goods in boxes. Within a few months Mother was to leave this job and obtained a better paying position with the Woonsocket Rubber Company.

Before telling Mother's story at the rubber company, I should give the reader a short history of the rubber industry in Woonsocket. Next to the textile industry, the rubber industry was the second major employer in the Woonsocket area. The Woonsocket Rubber Company (WRC) was initially formed in the 1870s to produce rubber for the Bailey Wringing Machine Company, which was also located in Woonsocket. The WRC produced a fine grade of rubber which was used to make the cylindrical-shaped clothes wringers of the time. From this beginning, the WRC expanded into other rubber products and became a major manufacturer of rubber boots and shoe products. The great success of the WRC was due mainly to its owner and president, Joseph Banigan, an Irish immigrant. Starting a rubber company in Massachusetts, Banigan expanded to Woonsocket and built a large mill which was called The Alice Mill (named after one of Banigan's daughters). In 1894, the WRC was sold to the US Rubber Company and a couple of years later Banigan left the company entirely.

Mother started working at the Alice Mill in 1917, just in the period when the company was adding employees to meet it's government contracts for World War I. She was just one of hundreds of girls who were producing rubber boots for the army. When

Banigan was president, he naturally employed many Irish workers, but by Mother's time, the predominant ethnic group was French Canadians. Of course the Irish were still well represented as well as small minorities of other ethnic groups. Mother tells the story of the difficult times a young German girl was given by her co-workers. Mother was working at the Alice Mill on Armistice Day, November 11, 1918 and she recalls that when word was spread throughout the plant, the management gave the workers the day off. All of Woonsocket and the Alice Mill workers held a mass rally in downtown Woonsocket where they burned the Kaiser in effigy.

Mother was working at the WRC in 1919 and continued to live at home with her father, siblings and stepmother. Her co-workers at the Alice Mill used to kid her about being the mill owner's daughter because of her name. She was relatively content working at the Alice Mill but over time was becoming increasingly fatigued by the lack of a proper diet, the constant harrassment at home and the press for increased production of boots at work. One day her supervisor at work scolded her for not having made enough boots. Not being one to tolerate abuse or fools, Mother grabed the boots she was working on and threw them at her supervisor's feet and walked off her job, not to return.

A few days later, she encounted a girlfriend while she was downtown. Noticing how skinny and drawn Mother was and her obvious depression, the girl asked her what was the matter. Mother proceeded to tell her friend about her terrible home life and that she had quit her job. Her friend said that she had a perfect solution for Mother. It seems that Mother's friend was leaving her job as a nanny for an affluent family with three young boys and that she would be happy to recommend Mother for the job. Since the nanny lived with the family, it would solve both of Mother's problems in that it would give her a good job and also a decent place to live. Seeing the logic of her friend's advice, Mother went for an interview with "the lady of the house" and got the position.

Thus began over three years of Mother's happy employment

with the Sadwin family. Mother's employer, Louis Sadwin, was the owner of a curtain manufacturing and a curtain retailing store, both in Woonsocket. Though the Sadwins were Jewish, both Louis and his wife Edythe spoke French fluently. As previously mentioned, most people in any kind of retail trade in Woonsocket spoke French even if they were not French Canadian themselves. Edythe Finstein Sadwin had been educated in a French speaking school in Fall River, Massachusetts and her knowledge of French was a valuable asset to her husband's businesses. At the time Mother went to work for the Sadwins, they had three sons (Harold, Sherwood, and Robert) and they shortly thereafter had another son named Daniel. Mother was only responsible for the care of the first three sons and Mrs. Sadwin took care of the baby. From the very beginning, Mother and the Sadwins had an excellent relationship. Though Mother was still in her teens, she had a natural way with children. Having grown up in a large family herself and having had the example of a firm but kindly father, she seems to have easily adapted to being a nanny. Like her father, I imagine she was firm but loving and over time she came to love the boys as they came to love her. Within a short time, she came to be looked upon as one of the family. She naturally had her own room which she certainly did not have in her stepmother's house. Her salary was not large, but it included room and board. Mr. Sadwin would buy the latest fashions for Mrs. Sadwin on his business trips to New York and often bought fashionable gifts for Mother as well. Mrs. Sadwin, for her part, treated Mother in a motherly manner and even insisted on meeting and passing opinions and advice on any person Mother dated. On one occasion, Mother brought home an Irish salesman she had met and Mrs. Sadwin advised her to date only suitable French Canadians. She told Mother that she was certain that this is what Mother's father would wish.

    Mother, of course, had time off from her duties but if she had occasion to be out late, Mrs. Sadwin insisted and paid for Mother to take a taxi home. Before long Mother became the best fed and best dressed of all her girlfriends, and her appearance and her spirits improved considerably. It was in this period that Mother became totally proficient in English as she was in French. Up until this time, all of her schooling, her friends and her home life had been spent using the French language. Mother even began to learn a good deal of Hebrew in the Sadwin home.

In 1919, the Tellier family had a tragic loss. Mother's older sister Diana Tellier died on October 16, 1919. She was twenty years, two months and six days old. Mother said that she had caught a cold when she went swimming at a picinic given by St. Ann's Church for "The Children of Mary". She never recovered from the cold and died in the fall. It was a great loss for all the family, and in particular for my mother who still speaks sadly about the event over eighty years later. Although all of the Tellier children were fairly attractive and handsome, Diana was absolutely beautiful. Since my early years, I have always been fascinated by a portrait picture of Diana that Mother has in the family album. She was probably eighteen or nineteen years old at the time with long shiny brown hair, perfectly delicate features and intense dark eyes. She has an almost sad expression on her face, as if she somehow knew that a tragedy was to shortly befall her; a "Mona Lisa" type of appearance, if you will. It is a melancholy story; she died on the brink of life

By 1921, all of the Tellier children had left Grandfather and his wife's home. After Diana's death and Mother's departure, only Uncle Alphonse and Aunt Marie Rose remained. Like Mother, Uncle Alphonse could no longer stand life at home and he went to live with a friend named Noe Tessier. Aunt Marie Rose went to live with a married sister, Aunt Marie Ann. Only Grandfather was left to suffer the abuses of a failed marriage.

Sometime around 1922, Mother had occasion to go to a benefit dance at the Woonsocket State Armory building on South Main Street. Mother loved to dance and she and her girlfriends went dancing at every available opportunity. Mother was especially looking forward to this dance because a well known entertainer of the era named Monty Blue was going to be there. In preparation for the event, Mother went to Providence to buy a new dress and she also purchased a large brooch for her hair. Being a short girl, just five feet one inch tall with a fine figure, a cute face and long brown hair, she surely must have made a pleasing appearance. During the course of the evening, she and her girlfriend were standing on one side of the dance floor when her friend called her attention to a handsome guy on the other side of the floor who she said kept staring at her. Before long, the fellow began walking across the floor towards them and Mother's friend said "It looks like he is coming to ask me for a dance.". Within a few moments, the guy was standing in front of the girls and he asked Mother for a dance. Surprised, Mother looked at her friend for direction and her friend said "Go ahead Alice, dance.". Well, Mother and this fellow danced the rest of the evening together. The reader may have already guessed the identity of the young man. He was named Herve Brunelle and he was to become my father.

After their first meeting, Mother and Father began seeing each other quite regularly. After a few dates, and per Mrs. Sadwin's wish, Mother introduced Father to the Sadwin's. As Mother expected, Mrs. Sadwin gave Father an unqualified approval. Since Father was French Canadian (and naturally Catholic) and he came from a "good" Manville family, he met all of the basic criteria for an acceptable boyfriend. Beyond this, however, Mrs. Sadwin came to like Father personally. When Grandfather Tellier came to know Father, he also liked him.

CHAPTER 8

A Union of the Descendents 1923 - 1930

A Sad Departure

Sometime in 1923 Mother sadly decided to leave Mrs. Sadwin's employ. I say "sadly" because in over three years of her stay at the Sadwin's, she had become very fond of Mrs. Sadwin and the entire family. Mrs. Sadwin had always been very kind to Mother and had provided a home for her when she most needed it. Additionally, I believe (although I don't think Mother was conscious of it) that Mother came to look upon Mrs. Sadwin as a surrogate mother. Having been without her own mother since the age of three, Mother certainly needed support and guidance in her teen years when she went to work for the Sadwins. Ironically, the main reason for Mother's departure from the Sadwins was my father, who Mrs. Sadwin always liked. Having "gone steady" with each other for over a year, Mother and Father were planning on getting married. Though Mother was happy at the Sadwins, she was finding it increasingly difficult to find free time to spend with Father. Mother was now often taking care of the four boys. (Mrs. Sadwin subsequently also had a daughter named Thelma, but this was after Mother's departure.) Also, Mother wanted to save money for her wedding.

Mother's sister, Marie Ann offered Mother a solution to her problems. She extended Mother the invitation to come live with her and her husband, Jules Hantis, at their apartment in the Bernon District of Woonsocket. In this way, she could have a good home and get a higher paying job to save money. Also, all of Mother's evenings would now be free for her to see Father. Mother left Mrs. Sadwin's employ on good terms, though Mrs. Sadwin was sorry to see her leave

Surprisingly, Mother's new job was back at the Woonsocket Rubber Company which she had abruptly quit over three years before. Apparently the Personnel Department had not made note of how Mother had left. I suspect, however, that Mother's future brother-in law, Ernest Villeneuve, had spoken up for her and gotten her the job. Ernest was a supervisor at the Alice Mill and was dating Mother's sister Marie Rose (they would marry in 1925). Mother returned to the Alice Mill and worked there until her marriage.

A Happy Union

On July 7, 1924 Marie Antoinette Alice Tellier, the tenth generation granddaughter of Jean Baptiste LeTellier dit LaFortune, married Herve Joseph Brunelle, the ninth generation grandson of Hilaire Limousin dit Beaufort. They were married in the French Canadian Precious Blood Church which is the parish church of the Bernon District. Uncle Romeo Brunelle supplied the transportation to and from the church with his new Packard automobile.

Precious Blood was a large red brick church built in 1909 that had (and still has) an eight foot gold-leafed cross on it's tower. Being a large church, Mother's walk down it's long aisle must have seemed endless to a nervous bride. After the wedding, they must have gone to a local photographer to have formal pictures taken. A large, ornately framed, oval wedding portrait of Mother and Father hung on our wall for years when I was young, until it was finally relegated to a storage closet in the 1950's. I do not think this relegation was a concession to modern times as much as it was that Mother was not happy about her appearance in the picture. I personally always thought that they looked handsome together and I am happy to report that the picture now hangs proudly on my sister's parlor wall.

However, the photographs that really tell the story of my parent's wedding day are not the studio photographs but the "Brownie" camera snapshots that were taken in front of Aunt Marie Ann's house. The building was a typical Woonsocket three story wooden apartment house with long expanses of open porches on each floor. Various group shots were taken in the front of the entrance steps. Some are male only shots of Father with his friends, brothers, brothers-in-law and both my grandfathers. Others are female only shots of Mother with her sisters, sisters-in-law, friends and Grandmother Brunelle. There are also a couple of photos of my parents and both my grandfathers. The interesting picture to me, however, is a group photograph of my parents, my grandfathers, my grandmother Brunelle and another lady who I did not recognize When I asked Mother who this lady was, she said it was her stepmother. As far as I can determine, it is the only picture of Grandfather's second wife in Tellier family possession. It specifically serves to tell me that Grandfather Joseph and his wife were still living together in July 1924.

Despite his reduced financial circumstances by 1924, Grandfather Tellier generously gave Mother a wedding present of a few hundred dollars. In today's dollars this would be equilavent to a few thousand dollars. Mother wisely resisted the newlywed's urge to spend the money immediately and rather put the money in a savings account. In the next chapter the reader will see why I say Mother acted wisely. In addition to the gift of money, Grandfather also gave Mother the Tellier family Singer sewing machine. This was a wise choice of gifts by grandfather as we will also see in the next chapter.

I have always wondered why Grandfather was so generous to Mother despite his own financial condition at the time of her marriage. Could it have been Grandfather's subconcious wish to compensate Mother for the loss of her happy home due to his remarriage? Possibly he felt guilty that he had unknowingly made the wrong decision in remarrying which had terrible adverse effects on his remaining family, particularly on his youngest surviving child, Mother. As I have said before in this story, the reader's guess is as good as mine. Surely though, it's an interesting question.

After the wedding, Mother and Father left on a week honeymoon to Newport, Rhode Island. They stayed in an ocean-front hotel that was located directly across the road from Easton's Beach. Years later when I had occasion to visit Grandmother Brunelle's family in Newport (the Lincourts) with my parents, I asked Mother where the hotel was. She replied that since it's location was vacant, it had probably been swept away in the devastating hurricane of 1938.

Herve and Alice Brunelle: 1924-1929

After their marriage, my parents went to live with my father's parents in Manville. Father was working as a textile weaver in the Manville Mills when he married and their residence in my grandparents home was a temporary one until Mother and he could find an apartment and other jobs, if necessary. After about six months, Father obtained a "weavers" job in Pawtucket, Rhode Island and then found an apartment in that city. Mother tells me that she did not mind the time she lived with her in-laws, rather she enjoyed it. She had the opportunity to know my grandparents well and to really get to like them. Grandfather was a very interesting man and Grandmother taught Mother many valuable lessons on how to be a good '"homemaker". Grandmother was a very gentle and shy lady and Mother said that though Father looked like his father, she could see many of Father's traits were gotten from Grandmother.

As gentle as Father was, he had a hobby at the time of his marriage which one would imagine was quite inconsistant with his gentle nature. That hobby was boxing. Since his late teen, Father was an amateur boxer who fought under the name "Kid Brown" (I imagine it was derived from the French meaning of his last name.). Apparently Mother was not happy with Father's hobby, and fearing injury to his quite handsome features, she finally prevailed on him to find some other interest. Possibly the reason Father was into boxing was that he was very interested in physical fitness and health related matters. Beliving in a strong healthy body, Father was also into eating properly. In terms of diet, cooking methods and vitamin supplements, he was decades ahead of the times which has now culiminated and produced the so called health enthusiats of the present generation. Father influenced Mother to be health minded and to change from the traditional French Canadian preference for pork products to food more palatable to Mother's unusually delicate stomach. I don't believe it took much convincing on Father's part because Mother had always said that the diet in her father's house, when she was a youngster, did not agree with her. Fortunately for Mother's digestion, she had gotten away from eating pork products. Being Jewish, the Sadwins did not eat pork. Father became increasingly impressed over the years with the teachings of a man named Bernarr MacFadden who published the "Physical Culture Magazine". Starting in the 1920's, MacFadden built a publishing empire based on good health periodicals, national health lectures and courses, and health based products.

On May 30,1925, Mother and Father had their first child, a girl who they named Constance. If Mother had found a job when they first moved to Pawtucket, she would have been in the position for only a short while. With the birth of Constance (Connie as she grew older), Mother now remained home to care for her child.

My brother Normand was born the next year on December 12, 1926. Having two children so early in their marriage, one suspects that the honeymoon was an abbreviated one. Before Normand was born, and knowing that they would need more room, my parents moved to a larger apartment in Central Falls the adjacent city to Pawtucket.

Sometime around 1930, Grandfather Tellier came to live with my parents in Central Falls. Having endured all of the hardships of a bad marriage, Grandfather left "his wife's" unhappy home. Of course being a Catholic, divorce was out of the question. Mother tells me that Grandfather had gone to the parish priest for guidance and though an annulment from the church was not possible, the priest agreed that Grandfather could no longer live with his wife. He could remain in good standing with the Catholic Church (go to mass, receive sacraments, etc.) as long as he didn't get a divorce.

I don't know if Grandfather came directly to live with Mother or if he went to live elsewhere first. One of Normand's earliest recollections is of Grandfather Tellier sitting at the family table at mealtime. Based on Normand's birth date of 1926 and adding three or four years, I would estimate Grandfather's arrival date as 1929 or 1930. Being a wise man and recognizing that living with his daughter's family made her life more difficult, Grandfather only remained for about a year. He then rented a room In Woonsocket which had been his home since coming to the United States. Also, this put him closer to all his other children and their families who all lived in the Woonsocket area.

CHAPTER 9

The Great Depression 1929-1939

Father Emulates Grandfather

In early 1929, having no way of knowing that desperate times were just around the corner, my father did what his own father had done just five years before; he purchased a new Chrysler automobile. It was not as grand a model as Grandfather had bought but was nonetheless a new car. As we will see further in this chapter, this automobile was not to become the "beloved Chrysler" that Grandfather's had become. Rather, it was to become "that detested Chrysler" as Mother so often referred to it in later years.

Father now had the luxury of commuting to work in his own vehicle rather than resorting to public conveyance. Unfortunately, this luxury was to be short lived because before many months, Father did not have a steady job to drive to.

In late October of 1929, the country entered what is now known as The Depression Era. On October 24, the so-called "Black Thursday", the New York Stock Exchange had the wildest day it had ever experienced with 12.8 million shares changing hands in a selling stampede. Prices across the board fell to disastrous levels. For the next five days prices continued to fall despite the best efforts of responsible bankers and businessmen to stop the fall. On Tuesday, October 29th, 16.4 million shares were traded and the great "Bull Market" of the previous four years was over. From the peak of the "Bull Market" in September 1929 to "Black Thursday", 32 billion dollars worth of equity had been wiped out.

I can say with certainty that Father did not lose one penny on the Stock Market plunge. Neither he nor probably most of the other French Canadians in Rhode Island were involved in stock speculation in the 1920's. French Canadian mill workers were salaried workers and Wall Street concerns were far from their minds. Making ends meet was their primary day-to-day concern. Of course, what happened on Wall Street in October 1929 was to affect the entire nation and quickly affected the textile industry in New England.

Early Depression Years

The Stock Market crash and its subsequent economic depression crippled the New England textile industry. By 1935, the unemployment rate for textile workers in Woonsocket was approximately 50% and many of those who did have jobs were only working part time. When you contrast this figure with the highest national unemployment rate of approximately 25% for the decade of the Depression (1929-1939), you get a measure of the severity of life in Rhode Island for my parents and other textile workers. Added to the loss of jobs during the Depression was the added factor that New England textile jobs, particularly in the cotton industry, had started to move to southern states in the decade of the 1920's. The reasons for this were basically threefold: lower worker salaries in the south, employers' attempts to get away from developing trade unions in the Northeast, and the search for cheaper overhead costs (heating and electric costs, property costs, lower taxes, etc.).

By 1930, the Woonsocket population had risen to approximately 50,000 and it is estimated that 70% of this number were French Canadians. Of course the majority of the Woonsocket workers were employed in the textile mills.

Though I don't know the statistics for other Rhode Island towns such as Central Falls where my family now lived, their numbers were surely just as bleak. Being the smallest U.S. state, Rhode Island towns were geographically very close to each other. Because of this, you could consider towns such as Woonsocket, Manville, Albion, Pawtucket, Central Falls, etc. as practically a part of one metropolitan area. Since the textile industry was predominat in all the towns, the chances of finding a textile job in any given town in the Depression were greatly diminished.

Other industries in Rhode Island also suffered in this period. The Alice Mill of The U.S . Rubber Company where my mother had worked before and after World War 1, was finally forced to close down. Many other businesses went bankrupt due to the hard economic times.

In those periods when my father was without a job, the family was literally kept from starvation and eviction by income from Mother's periodic employment. She fortunately was able to find occasional jobs as a "winder" in textile plants. Both Mother's and Father's jobs in the Depression were often only temporary positions. No other benefits, i.e., sick time, health insurance, vacation time, etc., came with these jobs. The employers were in the driver's seat. They reminded their workers that they were lucky to even have a job.

A little story my mother once told me concerning finding a job in the Depression clearly demonstrates the desperation and tenacity Mother felt in this period of her life. Being told by a friend that there might be a winder's position open in a small textile shop not far from her home, Mother went to inquire as early as she could the following morning. Upon arrival at the company, she was told that the job had just been filled and the woman who they had selected was already working in the shop. When Mother continued to sit in the waiting room, the company manager asked her "Madam, what are you doing?". Mother explained to the man that she really needed a job because she had two children at home and no money to feed them. She further explained that maybe they would find that the woman they had hired was inexperienced and unsatisfactory, in which case they might give her a chance at the position. Wisely recognizing Mother's determination to not move from her seat, the man said "Do as you wish lady." and left the room. Before the end of the morning, and with my mother still in the waiting room, the manager returned and told her it appeared the lady they selected did not know how to do the job. He then advised her that she could try out for the job immediately and if she demonstrated experience and skill, they would hire her. Mother passed the afternoon test and was hired by the now- impressed company manager.

As mentioned earlier in this chapter, Mother bitterly complained about Father's Chrysler automobile. This complaint was based on the fact that our family could not apply for or receive public assistance because we owned an automobile. In actual matter of fact, there was little if any assistance available to the thousands of poor people in this period. Mother overlooked the fact that Father's automobile gave him mobility to search a larger area for a job. During one extended period of time, the auto allowed Father to work and room in a distant town in Rhode Island and come home to Central Falls on weekends. It is easy for this author to be objective with the hindsight of seven decades and one must excuse Mother's inability to see all aspects of a difficult situation.

My mother's other complaint against the Chrysler was that Father was still making time payments on the car. They had used a portion of Grandfather Tellier's wedding gift of money to make a down payment and had financed the balance of the price. Father, of course, did not wish to default on the car and lose everything he had paid for it. Mother, on the other hand, took the position that she barely had money for food and rent, never mind money for car payments. Clearly both their arguments were valid. It is interesting to look back to this desperate period in my parent's early married life and realize how their trials and tribulations affected their views and philosophy in later life. For the rest of their lives after the Depression, they never purchased anything on time. They would not even agree to purchase a house if it required a mortgage.

Another concern that Mother had was Father's involvement with textile unions. Going back to the 1920's, Father had concluded that the only protection an individual worker had against management was to unionize and that there was strength and security in numbers. The union movement in Rhode Island had begun in earnest in the 1920's and by the 1930's the Independent Textile Union (ITU) had gained considerable membership and strength. If there was a union to join at a given job, Father happily joined and became an active member. Throughout his life, he continued to be a dedicated advocate of unions. On some jobs, he became a union shop steward and on others, where there was no union, he often assumed the role of unofficial union organizer. Of course this did not exactly endear him to management and Mother was convinced that it cost Father any number of jobs. This was a valid concern on Mother's part since finding and keeping a job in the Depression was difficult enough without the union sympathizer's handicap.

When unemployed and he could not find a textile job, Father, as did many others in the Depression, tried door-to-door salesman jobs. These attempts met with complete failure. I believe the reason was twofold: no one had any money to buy anything and Father, with his basically shy disposition, did not have the aggressive nature needed to sell anything in a depressed economy.

Surely these were terrible times for my parents and the majority of the people in the nation. With two young children to feed and often little or no food in the house, Mother gave whatever food she had to my sister Connie and my brother Normand. When they could no longer afford the rent, they moved to a smaller, cheaper apartment in Central Falls.

By 1932, Mother was completely run down and exhausted. She had lost considerable weight and her resistance to any number of physical ailments was nonexistent. It was at this time when she had a serious medical emergency which almost claimed her life. She never made it completely clear to me what caused the problem (maybe she never knew), but the symptoms were high fever and bleeding (possibly a continuation of her period). When it became obvious that the problem was serious, Father called the doctor and he came to the house (doctors still made house calls at this time). When the doctor arrived, he sullenly stated to Father "Why have you waited so long, this woman is half dead." He prescribed some medication and a diet of food for Mother and then left. When Father examined the "heavy" foods that the doctor had recommended, he bravely said to Mother that he believed that if her sickness did not kill her, this diet would. He then proposed that Mother go on a diet of fruit juices only, (orange juice, etc.) and see what effect it would have. As mentioned previously, Father, from a very early age, had subscribed to the eating and health principles of the early health practitioners such as Bernarr Macfadden, and had already done much reading on the subject. In any case, Mother trusted Father's opinion over the doctor's and for the next few days proceeded to starve the sickness while drinking juices only. Within a week Mother stopped bleeding and her temperature returned to normal. When the doctor finally made his follow-up house call, he seemed amazed to find mother weak, but otherwise feeling well. Both Mother and Father said nothing to the doctor, allowing him to take satisfaction in the wisdom of his professional skills.

If Mother's recovery was viewed as a vindication of my father's health concepts or as a verification of her doctor's medical skills, it may also have been received as a miraculous recovery by my mother's sister, Marie Rose. The reason why I think Aunt Rose (the first names of Marie of all my aunts were never used because of the confusion using them would cause) may have felt the recovery was "miraculous" is related to the story of her husband's French Canadian heritage. As previously mentioned, Aunt Rose married Ernest Villeneuve a year after my mother got married. In addition to now being her brother-in-law, Ernest was a friend from Mother's Alice Mill days. Being only one year younger than Aunt Rose, Mother was closer to Rose than any of her other siblings. After both sisters were married, my parents and Uncle Ernest and Aunt Rose used to "hang out" together whenever they had the opportunity. When Aunt Rose become aware that Mother was seriously ill, she gave Mother a St. Joseph's medal and told her that they and Frere (Brother) Andre were praying for her recovery. Uncle Ernest was the great nephew of Frere Andre (1846-1937) who was a religious brother of an order in Montreal (Ernest's mother was the niece of Frere Andre.). Prior to World War 1, Frere Andre had asked his religious superiors for valuable church property on Mount Royal overlooking Montreal. He wished to build a church venerating St Joseph, who is the Patron Saint of Canada. When it became apparent to the church hierarchy that Frere Andre had a huge following of Laity due to numerous medical cures that were attributed to Frere Andre's intercession to St. Joseph, they gave him permission to start building his church. Between 1917 and the 1930's, many documented cures were to occur and Frere Andre was to raise the funds to build St. Joseph's Oratory on Mount Royal. Frere Andre became nationally famous in the United States as well as Canada and he made several fundraising trips to the U.S. in the 1920's and 1930's. Whenever he visited Rhode Island, he would stay with Aunt Rose and Uncle Ernest.

    I cannot leave the subject of Frere Andre and Uncle Ernest without telling another story which concerns their family's relationship to the Tellier family. By another strange coincidence of history, Frere Andre's original ancestor in New France was also a French soldier in the same regiment as the Tellier and Brunelle ancestors and they all arrived in 1665. Frere Andre's secular (real) name was Alfred Bessette and his ancestor's name was Jean Besset dit Brisetout (1642-1707). Also, like my Brunelle maternal ancestor, Uncle Ernest's first maternal ancestor (Jean Besset's wife) was a Fille du Roi. Her name was Anne Seigneur (1649- 1733).

The Years 1933-1937

In early 1933, my family was living on the second floor of a modest two story colonial style house on Fuller Avenue in Central Falls. My sister Connie was eight years old and brother Normand was seven. I am not certain if both, or either, were in parochial school in 1933. Since starting school, both had been transferred between parochial and public schools due to our changes of residence and also our difficult financial circumstances. As anyone who has ever had children in parochial schools will attest, parochial schools are more costly. Though my parents favored parochial schools, it was not always possible to send Connie and Normand to them.

Not long after her illness in 1932, Mother became pregnant. On June 4,1933 she celebrated her 30th birthday, and four days later my parents had their third child, a boy, who was born at home. Mother vividly recalls that it was an extremely hot day in Rhode Island and had broken the temperature record for June 8th. (This record was not broken again until the 1980's.) In these times it was usual for children to be born at home rather than in the hospital and both Connie and Normand were born in our apartments in Pawtucket and Central Falls , respectively. Home birthing was a custom that did not really change until the 1940's. Though it was traditionally driven, clearly the hard economic times of the depression made hospital births prohibitive for many people in the 1930's. Given my mother's recent illness, I believe that my parents had considerable anxiety about the possible health of their newborn but by the goodness of God their son was born apparently normal. They named him Joseph Robert Camille Brunelle and as I believe the readers of this story already suspect, this particular Joseph Brunelle is the author of this family history.

In the paragraph describing my mother's health crisis, I gave three opinions on why Mother survived: my parents view, the doctor's view and my Aunt Rose's view. I trust the reader will indulge me and allow the author's view. I have given much thought to this question over my lifetime. I honestly believe that Mother's survival under difficult and almost primitive conditions, by the standards of today's medical knowledge, was pre-ordained. Whether by God, faith, fate, or destiny depends on one's perspective. There can be no doubt, however, that if Mother had not survived, I would not be here to tell this Tellier/Brunelle story.

If the reader will further indulge me, we can take this question of existence one more step, at least as far as the Tellier family is concerned. If our original ancestor, Jean Baptiste Letellier, had not survived to have three wives and two families, then his last child, Joseph Tellier from whom we are all descended, would never have been born. Jean was fifty eight years old when his last child Joseph was born and he died but four years later. Surely there is a Grand Design to the universe and life is more than a genealogical game of chance.

If ever there was a pivotal and defining moment in history to be born, 1933 was surely that moment. It was the year in which three men came to political power who would dominate world, national and local history for the next twelve years (1933-1945). Of course these men would indirectly dominate my life as well, although I was clearly not aware of them for about the first eight or nine years of my life.

On the world scene, Adolf Hitler was appointed Chancellor of Germany on January 30,1933 by a reluctant President Von Hindenburg. The Nazis received 40% of the German vote in

July 1932 due to the dissatisfaction caused by the worldwide depression and the German bitterness resulting from the harsh reparations of World War 1 and the Treaty of Versailles.

In the United States, the Democratic Governor of New York, Franklin D. Roosevelt (FDR), was inaugurated President on March 4, 1933 on a raw windy day in Washington, D.C. He had defeated President Herbert Hoover by a vote of 22+ million to Hoover's 15+ million votes in November 1932. Clearly the Depression and desperate times of the last four years had convinced Americans that anyone was better than "do nothing Hoover". In Rhode Island, which had been Republican, there was a solid Democratic sweep and citizens of Woonsocket voted for FDR by a vote of two to one.

In New York City, Fiorello LaGuardia became mayor on a broad based Republican-Fusion ticket. He replaced former playboy Mayor Jimmy Walker who was forced to resign in 1932,by FDR, in the wake of a widespread corruption scandal in the city government. (Walker subsequently took a boat to Europe with his mistress to avoid possible prosecution.)

This then was the world, national and local scene for my first twelve years. Hitler, of course survived until May 1945, FDR was to be elected President four times, dying in April 1945, and LaGuardia was to serve three terms as Mayor of New York City, leaving office in 1945. Not intending to get ahead of my story, I will only say here that for the first dozen years of my life, I was under the politically naïve impression that all three politicians were appointed to their jobs for life (like the monarchs of old).

I believe my father probably voted for FDR. Things were so bad that a definite change was needed. Additionally, as Governor of New York, FDR had shown himself to be pro-union and in his campaign speeches had promised many social reforms (A New Deal) for the people, which he did attempt to implement when he became President. These were the things Father definitely favored and would have influenced his vote. However, I must admit to the reader that I am only speculating here. By the time I was old enough to have some understanding of politics, my father had turned away from FDR and had become anti Roosevelt. The reasons for this are complex but probably the basic reason is that by the Presidential election of 1935, the nation was still deeply in a depression and my family's economic circumstances had not improved at all. Mother and Father still struggled with the basics; putting food on the table and paying the rent. Mother was able to keep the family in clothing only because she had learned to sew. Using Grandfather Tellier's wedding present of the Singer sewing machine, she made all of the children's clothes as well as her own.

Father was a very proud man and he never asked his own father for help. Mother told me that on one occasion Grandfather Brunelle was in the area and he decided to stop by our house for a short visit. Father was not home at the time. On seeing how desperate things were (my mother didn't have any food in the house), he gave Mother a few dollars and told her not to tell Father which she never did. Psychologically, the deprivations of the Depression affected my sister more than my brother or myself. Because of my age, I didn't know or understand what poor was. Normand was old enough to understand but because of his easy going nature, our situation did not seem to affect him. Mother often said that the smallest things satisfied Normand. Connie on the other hand was sensitive and "high strung" and was deeply affected. Well into adulthood, I heard her remind Mother about the substandard clothes she was forced to wear to school. I take it Connie was referring to Mother's homemade clothes which were probably superior to (but maybe different than) what the other children were wearing. I feel the criticism was surely unfair to Mother but it serves to demonstrate the deep psychological scars the Depression left on those who lived through it.

The family continued to struggle with life in Central Falls. By 1937, my father felt that he had enough of being unemployed and looking for jobs that did not exist. It happens that sometime in the middle of the 1930', Father's oldest sister, Aunt Bertha, had migrated to New York City and was employed in a restaurant as a waitress (Aunt Bertha had married in the 1920's and was now separated or divorced.). She had rented a large (six room) apartment in Long Island City, Queens, overlooking Manhattan and would make a short subway commute to her job in Manhattan. To supplement her income and help pay for the rent, she rented a couple of bedrooms to boarders. In1937 Father decided to move to Aunt Bertha's and look for a job in the New York City area. Before leaving he put his Chrysler up on blocks next to Grandfather Brunelle's garage in Manville (Grandfather still had his own Chrysler in the garage.). Saying his good-byes to Mother and we children, he boarded the New Haven Railroad to New York where Aunt Bertha met him at Grand Central Station. Aunt Bertha's apartment was only three stops from the Grand Central subway station on the Flushing Line of the Independent Rapid Transit (I.R.T.). The Court Square Station was the first elevated station after the train exited the tunnel under the East River.

Within a short time, Father found a "weavers" position in the local Long Island City area. As the textile industry in New England was disappearing in the 1920's and 30's, numerous smaller textile shops continued to survive in areas such as New York City and Patterson, New Jersey. Being close to the garment industry in mid town Manhattan, there was still a demand for clothing as well as household fabrics. Additionally, Patterson was still a major silk manufacturing area and would remain so well into the 1940's.

Living frugally, Father was able to eat, pay his rent to his sister and send money home to Mother in Central Falls. (A year or so after I was born the family had moved to a larger apartment on Illinois Street, also in Central Falls.) Father was even able to save commuting expenses to work since his job was within walking distance to Aunt Bertha's.

Father's brother, Romeo Brunelle, also moved into Aunt

Bertha's apartment in this period. Romeo was also a textile weaver in Rhode Island and like Father was unable to find work. He had a wife, Aunt Sue, and three daughters (he subsequently had another daughter), who remained in Rhode Island. After he found a job in New York, he sent money to his family back home. Unlike Father, Uncle Romeo did not remain in New York. Aunt Sue advised him to come home because they had found him a good job. Quitting his job, Uncle Romeo returned to Rhode Island where he was greeted by a happy family but no job. Probably it had been a ruse by Aunt Sue to get Uncle Romeo to return home.

Another of father's siblings came to New York City in this period. Uncle Eugene (Gene) Brunelle and his wife Beatrice (Aunt Bea) came to live in Flatbush, Brooklyn when Uncle Gene got a job working in an electric power plant for the Consolidated Edison Company. As the reader may recall, Uncle Gene was the youngest Brunelle son and had received the benefit of a technical school education. Additionally, he and Aunt Bea had no children at this time so the move was easier and permanent.

It is interesting to note that while three of my father's family attempted to escape the poverty in Rhode Island during the Depression, none of my mother's Tellier family tried to leave. Possibly this was due to the fact that Mother's siblings had much larger families than the Brunelles. This would certainly have made it more difficult for the Tellier fathers to leave home, even temporarily. I also suspect that the Brunelle children were more cosmopolitan than the provincial Tellier children. The Brunelle children had been exposed to more of the world, i.e., musical instruction, cars, etc., than the Telliers and this would have better prepared them for life in "the big city"'. It is an interesting thought and I must confess to the reader that it never crossed my mind until this very moment.

CHAPTER **10**

A New Beginning 1938-1939

Mother Joins Father

By early spring of 1938 my parents had saved enough money to plan for Mother and we children to move to New York City. I do not know if this now permanent move had been contemplated or planned at the outset of my father's move to New York or if the decision just evolved over a period of time. I do know that Mother was not especially happy about leaving all of her family in Rhode Island. I suspect that Father's initial move to New York was solely a move of expediency (he couldn't find a job in Rhode Island), and then the loneliness of separation dictated that the family would eventually join Father.

However, before telling the story of our move I must tell the reader one unique, inexpensive method of communication my parents had developed between New York and Rhode Island. In the depression year of 1938 a telephone was a luxury that average families could not afford. Though I am sure they communicated by letter, I am sure that they also communicated in another rather unique way. As previously mentioned, after 1935 Father had pretty much turned away from FDR and his Democratic party. Father was now experimenting with political options and by 1937 he was exploring the ideas of a Catholic priest from Royal Oak, Michigan. This priest's name was Father Coughlin and he had developed his own political following via a nationally broadcasted radio program and a national weekly periodical called "Social Justice". Father had subscribed to this weekly while he was living in Rhode Island and long after he moved to New York City they were still sending it to our address at 316 Illinois Street, Central Falls, Rhode Island. What Mother would do is put a forwarding address of 45-17 21st Street, Long Island City, New York and gave it back to the postman without additional postage, and "lo and behold" it would be sent to New York City. Inside the periodical, Mother would write little messages to Father. One significant message was inscribed on page 19 of the March 21, 1938 "Social Justice". Mother's message in pencil reads as follows:

Dear Harvey,

Thanks for the money. I'm in a hurry this week as I'm housecleaning and sewing for the spring but I will write in a day or so. Please write and tell me if you want me to go or not next week. You know it takes a lot of money to go to New York, but anyway I will write again.

Alice

Just a great message from the past. I discovered it in the basement of my parents house on one of my attempts to clean up the basement in the 1980s. Father had saved magazines in the basement which went back to the 1930s. I happened to turn to page 19 and discovered this little treasure which as the reader can see told me such a great story about my parents.

I imagine my mother did visit father in April and they planned for the family to move to New York in May. With the help of her family, Mother packed the clothing she was going to take to New York and put the rest of our household items, furniture, kitchen stove and utensils, etc. (14 years of household accumulation) into storage in Central Falls.

On May 5, 1938, Mother, Norman, Connie and myself boarded a bus in Providence and traveled to New York City. My sister Connie has recalled the exact date these many years later because May 30 was her birthday. We moved into Aunt Bertha's apartment on 21st Street in Long Island City (LIC). It was quite an elegant circa 1900 apartment building of five stories, fronted by a large bay window which extended the entire height of the building. The apartment was on the top floor and the bay windows faced and had a beautiful, unobstructed view of the east side of Manhattan. This section of LIC is about in line with 42nd Street in Manhattan and the now eight year old art deco Chrysler building featured prominently in our view. Also visible was the seven year old Empire State building and the large office buildings further south in downtown Manhattan.

Since the grammar school year is not complete until the end of June, my parents enrolled both Connie and Norman in the nearby Queens Public School No. 1 (P.S.1) which was within a two block walking distance from our apartment. They were to remain in P.S.1 only for the two month remainder for the 1938 spring term.

I was not to turn five until June 8, 1938 so my parents waited until summer to enroll me in the parochial school at St. Mary's Church which was about ¾ of a mile from our apartment. At this time, they also enrolled both Normand and Connie in St. Mary's School. Though Connie is a year older than Normand, they were both enrolled in the same grade due to some confusion in the transfer process. For this reason both Normand and Connie were to subsequently graduate from St. Mary's school at the same time in June, 1941.

I am advised that I spoke mostly French when we moved to New York, so I imagine I had a quick learn to get up to speed with the English language. The nuns at St. Mary's were a French Order and I wonder if my first grade teacher helped me in this regard. My memory is very sketchy for this early period of my life. I do remember that the corporal punishment of children in the parochial school system was still in existence and I, as do many other people, still remember being forced to put my hand out to be hit by a couple of skinny wooden rulers held together by rubber bands. Actually I don't remember this punishment being as bad as the intimidation presented by the policy of having to raise your hand to get permission to go to the bathroom. I recall on one occasion having to sit in my seat in my wet short pants near the end of the school day because I was too scared to ask for permission to leave the room. Fortunately I was not detected and I didn't have the indignity of being laughed at by the other children.

St. Mary's had only one lay teacher and her name was Miss Kelly. The rest of the teachers were nuns. Miss Kelly must have been a real terror because all of the students who had passed the sixth grade (which Miss Kelly taught) used to say "Wait until you get to Miss Kelly's class.." Apparently Miss Kelly's discipline made the nuns seem like Mother Theresa by comparison. This is a frightening thought to me even as I write this story today. Fortunately I never reached sixth grade in St. Mary's School since I was transferred to P.S.1 when Normand and Connie graduated from St. Mary's.

Sometime in 1939, my parents found a third floor rental apartment in a three story brownstone building two blocks from Aunt Bertha's place. I believe our move from Aunt Bertha's was amicable but my Mom told me in later years that she naturally wanted her own place. Our furniture and possessions were taken out of storage in Central Falls and shipped to our new home on 45th Avenue. The apartment was in a brownstone that had been built in 1889 by a local builder and property owner whose name was Newland VanRiper. He lived in a one family brownstone two buildings down from our building and was maybe in his 70's at this time. In addition to our building, he also owned the three story brownstones on either side of our building and three other old brownstones on Jackson Avenue which was just around the corner from our new house. His family were of prominent Dutch ancestry who had populated New York when it was New Amsterdam. He, his father and his brother owned a construction company and had built our house as well as all the other buildings previously described. He was the sole remaining member of his family and was living on rental income and his family estate.

CHAPTER **11**

WORLD WAR II 1939 – 1945

The summer of 1939 saw the opening of the New York World's Fair at Flushing Meadows, Queens, N.Y. Getting to the The Fair was very easy from our house in Long Island City since the elevated Independent Rapid Transit (IRT) subway line that ran around the corner from our house (Court Square Station) ran through Queens directly to Flushing Meadows. We were to have much company visiting us that summer and the summer of 1940. Most were Mother's family members from Rhode Island and my parents would put them up in our apartment. Many temporary mattresses were placed on the floor in the back living room and the front parlor during the course of these stays. Mom and Dad would buy groups of tickets to The Fair and give the visitors tours of all the fair sites. Mother also provided meals for the visitors. Years later, I asked her if she ever got tired from all the company and she said, on the contrary, she enjoyed seeing her family. Since my parents had very few opportunities to visit Rhode Island, at least this was a substitute.

The few times we did return to Rhode Island were usually on the occasions of weddings and deaths. Dad's father Arsene Brunelle died in 1940 at the age of 70. He had been ill for a few years before he died and Grandma Brunelle had taken care of him as best as she could. The wake took place in the Manville R.I. house front parlor and it made a great impression on me since it was the first funeral I had ever attended. We had visited Manville the previous year and Grandfather had generously given me a shiny 50 cent piece. At that time he was relegated to a wheel chair and I remember Grandfather had a hospital bed in a downstairs bedroom next to the kitchen. I found out from Father years later how significant the 50 cent gift to me was. Grandfather's illness was before the days of medical coverage for the elderly and his illness had exhausted my grandparents resources. Before he left, my father had given Grandfather a few dollars and when he died, Grandmother discovered the money pined to Grandfather's housecoat.

Some of our visitors during this time also came as newlyweds. Cousin Rita Peloquin (Mother's niece) had married Gene Gaudin who had enlisted in the Army in 1940 and their visit was a combination honeymoon, visit to the World's Fair and a leave from the Army for Gene. Other cousins who were now in the military would visit when they were coming through New York to their various military duty stations.

President Roosevelt's administration realized that the European war which started in 1938 would eventually draw in the United States and had instituted a military draft. Coming from a large family of 53 first cousins in Mother's Tellier family alone, we were to provide much manpower to the war effort. Due to the lack of employment opportunities, many men including cousin Lucian Lebel (son of Annette Tellier Lebel) enlisted in the Army in the late 1930s, even before the draft was instituted. Lucian was stationed at Schofield Barracks, Hawaii on December 7, 1941 when the Japanese attacked Pearl Harbor. Lucian would see service in the Pacific theater throughout the war and safely survived to see the Japanese defeated. My brother Normand was a high school freshman on December 7, 1941 and he tells me that he had gone to the local movie house called the "Idle Hour" on that Sunday afternoon. Upon exiting the movie house and walking home, he was to hear that the Japanese had bombed our naval base in Hawaii. Little did he imagine as a 14 year old boy that he would be in the Army before the war was over.

In June 1941, Connie and Normand graduated from St. Mary's School and enrolled in the local Bryant High School. Bryant (named for the poet William Cullen Bryant of Roslyn, Long Island) was about ten blocks from our new residence on 45th Avenue and about a twenty minute walk to school. My parents withdrew me from St. Mary's school that summer and enrolled me in P.S.1 which was a much closer walk to school. Of course this was before the time when there was public busing of parochial school students. In fact, public busing was not even available to Connie and Normand for the public high school since they were considered within walking distance.

At the time of my transfer from St. Mary's Parochial School to public school in September 1941, I was entering grade 3B. A review of my report cards for grades 1A through grade 3A indicate that surprisingly my grades were quite good. In those days the school year was broken up into two grades per year (grade 1A, 1B, 2A, 2B, 3A, 3B etc.) I say surprisingly because I was really not fluent in English upon entering first grade, in fact, up to that point in my life I had spoken only French. Parochial schools could be quite difficult due to their heavy emphasis in the academics such as reading, writing and arithmetic as opposed to the heavier vocational emphasis of teaching in the public schools. My grade 2B marks in St. Mary's were as follows: Religion 90, English 96, Reading 83, Writing 85, Spelling 81, Arithmetic 95, drawing 95, music 95, hygiene 95, for an overall average of 91. St. Mary's principal Reverend Mother M. Consuela was stamped on the bottom of the report card and my teacher Sister M. Dominic had signed the card. My experience in grade 3B in P.S.1 is, after sixty seven years, (I write this account in the year 2008) a very distant memory. It is said that one tends to forget unpleasant experiences and remember pleasant thoughts. This may additionally contribute to my vague memory of the third grade. All I can recall of the requirements of 3B is our efforts in the crafts. One of our projects was that each one of us was to carve and paint a wooden Totem Pole about six inches high. Another was to contribute to building a miniature city made of paper and plaster. To this day, I am dexterously challenged. I can imagine what I was at seven or eight years old. Needless to say, I got "left back" and had to repeat grade 3B. The powers that be then decided to further humiliate me and pulled me out of a regular class and put me in a class for slow learners. After a couple of humiliating months, they thankfully realized the error of their ways and deposited me back in a regular class. The ironic feature of this entire sad experience was that the teacher who left me back was a second cousin to my best friend, Jay Moore, who lived across the street from our house on 45th Avenue.

Life in World War II changed for all Americans including the least of the citizens, the grammar school kids. I remember the tin can drives, the savings bonds stamp drives and all the other conservation and war efforts of school children. These efforts were even graded on our report cards. My 4B report card of February 1943 (Violet Ziebel teacher) gives me a barely passing grade of C for "War Effort". (I always suspected I had pacifist tendencies.) Possibly I didn't receive the money to buy the saving stamps to put in our savings bond books. These books were redeemed for $25.00 savings bonds upon entering $18.75 in stamps in the book.

Of course the war had major implications for my parents as well. I recall the food ration stamps that we would give to Mr. Begley, the grocer, for everything from meat to sugar and coffee. The problem was, there rarely was meat even if you had stamps. We always suspected that grocer Begley was charging more money under the table than the advertised price of meats. Stamps or no stamps, if you paid the inflated prices you got the meat. Fortunately for our family, Mother was very health minded and used to make great meatloaf with grain and other products that not only resembled meatloaf but tasted like it.

We did not have a car during the war years so we had no need for gas rationing or rubber tire stamps. Father had left his 1929 Chrysler up on blocks in Grandfather Brunelle's back yard in Manville, R.I. when he came to New York in 1937. Unfortunately for kids my age, manufacturers of products such as bicycles and toy trains were now producing war goods. Those people that already had these items would not sell them. I was not to receive a two wheel bicycle until Christmas 1947. When I was 14, Father saw an advertisement in the newspaper that Macy's had received a limited shipment of post war Columbia bikes so he went early and waited in line for my very first bicycle. It was my greatest Christmas present and I treasure it to this day (I still have it).

In 1942 Father left his textile weaving job and went to work as a "ship fitter" at the Kearny shipyard in New Jersey. Kearny was producing the so called "liberty ships" which were being mass produced in many shipyards building tankers to deliver war goods to the Allied countries (England, Russia, etc.) It was a long commute to New Jersey every day by way of subway and "path" train from Manhattan to Jersey. In addition to being a long commute, ship fitting was an extremely dangerous job. On one occasion a crane dropped a piece of steel which killed a fellow worker who was standing right next to Father. On another occasion he fell in a hole and severely cut a gash in his ankle for which he missed a number of work days. Even into his 70s Father was fearless when it came to heights. Assembling ships is like being a steelworker and requires ability to work high above the ground. I recall Father fearlessly painting our house on a three story ladder when he was in his early 70s.

Mother, with her health education and interests, obtained a job working in a health food store in Manhattan in the vicinity of Union Square. She worked behind the counter taking orders, preparing foods and performing waitress duties. She enjoyed her job and she certainly had the qualifications for the work. During and after the war, my parents continued their interest in "health" and attended many classes and lectures in nutrition, healthy eating and living.

By 1943 my brother Normand had gotten a part time job after school as an usher at the Radio City Music Hall in Manhattan. He would leave Bryant High School and take the subway directly from school to his job. In late 1943, Cousins Normand Peloquin and Arthur Tellier spent a few days at our house in Long Island City prior to entering the service. Brother Normand arranged for them to get free seats at the Music Hall and then took them for a tour backstage. Shortly afterward, Normand Peloquin (son of Marie Louise Tellier Peloquin) entered the Army and Arthur (son of Philbert Tellier) entered the Navy.

Military Service Begins

Of the fifty three grandchildren of Joseph Tellier (my first cousins), twenty seven were male. I have been able to identify more than one dozen cousins who served in the military in World War II. It is likely that there were others since there were more cousins that were old enough. The oldest cousins were of draft age for WWII, however, the younger cousins, myself included, were children and too young to serve. The younger cousins were to subsequently see service in the Korean, Vietnam and Cold War eras.

The WW II cousins served in most of the major theatres of the war from Europe in the west to the Philippines in the Pacific theatre. Some saw more than their share of combat, most notably Raymond Peloquin (Aunt Louise Tellier Peloquin's son) who landed on Omaha Beach on D-Day, June 6, 1944. It is a strange coincidence of history that when Raymond landed at Omaha Beach, he was only a few miles from the town of Coutances, Normandy which is where our original ancestor Jean Baptiste LeTellier was born in 1642.

Raymond was a Private First Class (PFC) in the U. S. Army

with the 329th Infantry Regiment, 83rd Infantry Division. His division spent 240 days in combat after D-Day. He was in the Ardennes Forest during The Battle of the Bulge when the Germans attempted to split the Allied Armies and reach the Meuse River in Belgium. Years later (in 1990), Raymond shared his thoughts for Christmas Eve December 24, 1944 as follows: "About 10 P.M., small Belgian village, deep snow, still snowing heavily. No moon. No stars. Very dark. No lighting of cigarettes. Kitchen crew arrives with chow: baked beans with a ladle of fruit cocktail thrown on top of the beans. Within a couple of minutes both beans and fruit welded, frozen together. But I was hungry and scraped this mess into my mouth. God, it was cold – frozen hands, frozen feet, frozen legs, frozen everything." Raymond went on "December 25, 1944 my foxhole roommate from Alabama says, 'Merry Christmas'. The sun came out that day".

While Raymond was fighting in Europe, his older brother PFC Gerald Peloquin's (son of Marie Louise Tellier Peloquin) duties centered on the transportation by railroad of German prisoners of war in New York.

The youngest Peloquin brother to serve in WW II was Normand Peloquin. While Raymond was freezing in a foxhole in Belgium, Normand had just completed basic training and infantry training in Alabama. He was then shipped to the Pacific Theatre and saw combat against the Japanese in the Philippine Islands.

Cousin Arthur Tellier (Uncle Philbert Tellier's son), who had visited us in New York with Normand Peloquin, went into the U.S. Navy and served in the Pacific aboard the battleship Colorado. Arthur's two brothers were in the Army in Europe by 1944. His brother Romeo Tellier saw service in Italy and Germany and was used as a French translator. Brother George Tellier started in London, England and eventually ended up in Germany by the end of the war. It is interesting to note that all my cousins were bi-lingual, knowing both English and French, and at least two were to be utilized by the Army as translators (George Tellier in

WWII and Normand Peloquin in the Vietnam War). PFC Raymond Peloquin found his French language skills very useful as his unit crossed France and Belgium. After the war was over, he had occasion to visit French friends in Normandy fifteen times.

My brother Normand Brunelle turned eighteen years old on December 12, 1944 and shortly thereafter enlisted in the Army Air Force. Due to the high turnover rate of young boys and men in the Usher Corps at Radio City Music Hall, Normand was by this time the head usher. His duties included seating of VIPs and scheduling of usher work schedules. Though he was a High School senior and not scheduled to graduate until June of 1945, the school had a program where they would give students diplomas early so they could enter the service.

Normand reported to basic training on April 4, 1945 in Texas and was to spend the majority of his Air Force career attending various technical schools. He started out going to B-29 aircraft engineer's school and then was transferred to B-29 engine maintenance school. Due to the constantly changing needs of the military and the ending of the war in August 1945, Normand was to end up doing engine maintenance on C-47 transport aircraft. He was to remain in the Air Force until October 14, 1946 at which time he returned to Bryant High School to take math and science regents courses he needed to enter college.

On Victory in Japan (V-J) day, August 14, 1945, Normand Brunelle was in a movie theatre in Times Square, New York City. He was home on leave and he and his girlfriend Nancy Mattson had gone into Manhattan to take in a movie and stage show at the famous Paramount Theatre. It is a coincidence that Normand was also in a movie house on December 7, 1941 when the war began.

My mother's brother Alphonse Tellier had one of his son's in WW II. His name is Robert Tellier and he served in the U.S. Navy. The other two boys in Uncle Alphonse's family were too young for service, however, his son Bernard was to serve in the Army during the Korean War.

Normand Tellier was the only one of the cousins to remain in the Army after WW II. After V-J Day, Normand was sent to Japan for occupation duty. By his nineteenth birthday, he was a Master Sergeant. By 1950 he was still stationed in Japan and was promoted to Warrant Officer. Between 1961 and 1966 he was an Intelligence Officer in France where his fluency in French was a great asset. Normand was to serve in the Army through the Korean War and served two tours of duty in Vietnam during that war. He served his last few years in Hawaii and was a French interpreter for the U.S. Army to Cambodian and Vietnamese VIPs. Normand retired from the Army on June 1, 1973, having served twenty nine years in the military.

Surely God looked after the cousins (Tellier, Lebel, Peloquin, Brunelle) in World War II. Not one cousin died in the war. We continued our good fortune through the next three wars (Korean, Vietnam, Cold Wars) with the younger generation of cousins; Roger Peloquin, Bernard Tellier and myself, Robert Brunelle, serving in the Korean War, Normand Peloquin serving in the Korean and Vietnam Wars and Gene Peloquin serving during the Cold War period in the late 1950s.

Although my sister Connie wasn't in the service in WW II, she did work for the Army the last year of the war. After high school she had taken a job at the Army Exchange in Manhattan (NYC). Her job was to take catalog orders from GI's and then make arrangements to have these purchases sent to the locations chosen by the servicemen.

The Tellier family had been in the war from the attack on Pearl Harbor (Lucian Lebel) through the "D-Day" invasion of Europe (Raymond Peloquin) to the battle against the Japanese in the Philippines (Normand Peloquin) to the final occupation of Japan after August, 1945 (Normand Peloquin) – quite a record of service to our country. Jean Baptiste LeTellier dit LaFortune and Hillaire Limousine dit Beaufort, the French soldiers who came to America in 1665 would have been proud of their descendants.

CHAPTER **12**

The Post War Years, 1946 – 1952

Dad Returns to Textile Work

The years immediately following World War II saw many changes in the Brunelle family life. With the end of the war, Dad left his ship fitting job in New Jersey and returned to his textile industry job as a weaver. While working at the shipyard, Dad was a union member of "The Industrial Union of Marine and Shipbuilding Workers of America – CIO". The date on his "Withdrawal Card" from the union was December 5, 1945. I believe the first weaver position he then took was at a small weaving shop in Jackson Heights, Queens. Since the elevated subway IRT line ran by our house and through Jackson Heights, he would have had a convenient, economical and short trip to work each day. Within a short while, Mother also obtained a job at this firm as a "Winder" which is what she had done in her Rhode Island textile days.

After a few years in Jackson Heights, Father moved on to still another textile position at a company called Scalamandre' Fabrics in Long Island City. This firm was a world famous fabric manufacturing company that made fine silk cloth for such places as the White House and other historic locations. Dad could now walk to work. I believe Mother left Jackson Heights when Father did and decided to remain at home for a while.

Sometime before 1950, Father moved on to still another textile position at a company called Geffen Textiles in L.I.C. This company was also within walking distance to our home. Dad was to be both a "weaver" and a "Fixer" in this job and was a valuable asset to the company since they received two talents for the price of one. Being a small, privately owned company, they did not need and could not afford a full time "Fixer".

Connie Brunelle

On March 30, 1946, exactly two months before her 21st birthday, my sister Connie married a local friend named Tom Gil. Tom was still in the U.S. Navy and was on a two month leave from his duty station on the island of Guam in the Pacific. Connie had known Tom for some time since he lived on 44th Drive, the next street over from our house on 45th Avenue. His parents were born in Spain and had individually immigrated to the U.S. in the 1920's. They had met in the U.S. and were married here. Prior to coming to this country, Mr. Cesare Gil had served in the Spanish Army.

Connie and Tom were married in St. Mary's Church in Long Island City which was both their home parish. Connie subsequently continued to live at home until Tom was discharged from the Navy. She had a number of jobs in Manhattan ranging from receptionist to payroll clerk. When Tom got out of the service, they lived in a number of places in Queens, none of which could be qualified as bona fide apartments. Apartments in New York City were in very short supply and impossible to obtain. Tom found a job at the Fisher Baking Company in Long Island City as a delivery route driver of cake and bread products to local Queens stores.

Two Important Events in 1947

From my personal perspective, two important events were to take place in 1947. In June, I graduated from grammar school (PS1) and enrolled in Long Island City High School (LICHS) for September. LICHS was actually the old renamed Bryant High School which Normand and Connie had attended. A new high school had been built in another part of Queens and given the name Bryant High School.

The other significant event for the year was the purchase of the house we were living in by my parents and Uncle Gene and Aunt Beatrice Brunelle. As previously mentioned, Dad's brother Gene and his wife had moved from Rhode Island and were now living in an apartment on Flatbush Avenue in Brooklyn. Mr. VanRiper, the owner and builder of the house (built in 1889) had decided to retire and sell all his real estate properties. Before putting his properties up for sale, he approached Dad telling him that he had been a good tenant and that he wished to give him an opportunity to make the first offer.

The price Mr. Riper was asking was reasonable in light of the fact that the building had not had much maintenance for years and needed a lot of work and updating. Dad approached Mom and told her that if we did not buy the house we would probably have to move once it was bought by a new owner. Mother said she didn't think we should buy a house that needed so much work. Dad reassured Mother by promising her that they would fix up and modernize the house.

The second obstacle to purchasing the house was the price. As mentioned previously, my parents had vowed to never again purchase anything on time since their sad experience in paying off a car during the depression. Mother would only buy the house if they could pay cash for the house and own it mortgage free. The war years had been financially good to the family and my parents, through frugal living, had been able to save a goodly amount of money, actually enough to pay half the price of the house.

Dad decided to approach his brother Gene to see if he would be interested in purchasing half the house. Through Uncle Gene did not wish to move into the house (the building has three apartments), he did decide that it would be a good investment from his point of view. Aunt Beatrice agreed and Mother finally agreed and the deal was consummated.

After the house was bought, Uncle Gene and Dad began to address the most pressing repair issues. Uncle Gene, who was working at a ConEdison Power Plant locally in L.I.C. would come over after work and he and Dad began working to restore the building (pouring new concrete support pillars in the basement, replacing the plumbing, etc.). It turned out to be a good arrangement since Uncle Gene was a very easy going and likeable gentlemen like my Dad and they got along and worked well together. Mother was content with the arrangement because one of her major concerns had been that she didn't want Dad to undertake such a huge house refurbishment by himself.

Normand Brunelle

After brother Normand was discharged from the military on October 14, 1946 he returned to L.I.C. High School to take courses which he required to enter college. He also signed up for the "52-20" program which the government had made available to veterans to help get them on their feet and transition to civilian life. What the "52-20" program meant was that veterans could receive $20.00 a week for 52 weeks to help them financially until they found a job or enrolled in college under the GI Bill program.

In September 1947 Norman enrolled as a freshman in the Mechanical Engineering curriculum at Brooklyn Polytechnic Institute located in downtown Brooklyn. As with the majority of veterans Normand probably would not have had the means to attend college without the GI Bill. Of all the benefits given to veterans, VA housing loans, 52-20 program, VA health benefits, etc., the college GI Bill was the greatest veteran's benefit ever offered and it allowed an entire generation of Americans to attend college.

As a result of the great demand created by millions of veterans entering college and trade schools within a short period after the war, schools became increasingly overwhelmed by the instant rush of new students. Class sizes often were too large for adequate instruction and demand for qualified professors often necessitated hiring adjunct instructors with little or no teaching experience.

Such was the case at Brooklyn Poly Tech and after a year of struggling with freshman courses, Normand and his fellow classmate and friend Jimmy Bunker (a local L.I.C. friend) transferred to Sampson College on Seneca Lake, New York hoping to find a more conducive environment for learning. Sampson College was a new college formed after WWII to help meet the new student rush and was a member of "The Associated Colleges of Upper New York". The college campus occupied the buildings and grounds of the former U.S. Naval Training facility that had trained thousands of naval recruits during the war. Normand purchased a 1935 Chevrolet Coupe (with rumble seat), loaded it with his possessions and he and Jimmy Bunker headed north to Sampson.

Normand was to spend his second year of college at Sampson and then was forced to transfer back to Brooklyn Polytech due to the apparent abrupt closing of Sampson College. Normand was to spend his third college year in Brooklyn and then his GI Bill benefits were exhausted. Benefits were based on the length of time you had spent in the service and Normand hadn't entered the service until near the end of the war. He promptly went job hunting and obtained a job as a mechanical draftsman at the Sperry Gyroscope Company in Great Neck, Long Island in early 1950.

On June 17, 1951, Normand married his girlfriend Nancy

Mattson in St. Mary's Church in L.I.C. Nancy was from Bayside, Queens and was at this time also working at Sperrys in the electrical assembly department. She was of German and Norwegian ancestry. Her father had been a Norwegian seaman in WWI and her mother was of first generation German ancestry. The newlyweds were able to find a garden apartment in Bayside, Queens which was not too far from their place of employment at Sperrys.

Bob Brunelle

My high school years at L.I.C. High School were in retrospect fairly uneventful. I entered high school in September 1947 and graduated in January 1951 with an academic diploma. I believe having been left back in third grade had actually negatively impacted my pride and sense of fairness and had inspired me to make up the time I had lost (one 5 month term). Consequently, I doubled up my courses so that I could skip a term in high school. By sixth grade I had enough credits to go into seventh grade and this pushed my eighth grade graduation up to January 1951 rather than June 1951. My standing out of a class of 234 students was I believe 32 from the top (not particularly brilliant but definitely respectable).

When I look back on the entire third grade failure affair, I believe my third grade teacher had done me a favor by making me so angry that I was determined from then on to excel in this academic business. Unfortunately one of the lessons in life is that there is always someone smarter. My good friend and classmate Eddie Sagara was smarter than I and he was the one who got to skip a grade in grammar school (PS1).

After my graduation in January 1951, I promptly went out and got a messenger job at the New York Daily News. My job was to go to the various customer stores such as Macys, etc. and pick up and bring back advertising copy for the daily paper. Finding a job as an 18 year old in 1951 was a real problem. The military draft was on and taking young men for the Korean war, therefore, companies did not see any use in hiring people who were about to be drafted.

After about three months at the News, I went to the personnel department to see if I could transfer to a more challenging lucrative job. The personnel man promptly put me in my place by telling me that some of my fellow messengers had college degrees and that my high school diploma didn't carry much weight. I would have to be patient and wait my turn in the messenger room. With my ego damaged, I decided to quit. When I told my boss in the messenger department I was quitting, he asked me if I had another job. (He was probably just three or so years older than myself and his last name was Flynn.) When I told him I had no job in mind, he said he had a friend who was in charge of the mailroom at Ford International on Park Avenue and 57th Street and that he would recommend me if I so wished (Years later I noticed that the CEO at the Daily News was a man named Flynn; I wonder if it was the same Flynn.)

Sometime in the spring of 1951 I started working at Ford International. Though it was just a mailroom job, it was actually a "high end" job in that Ford International was the executive office of the International Division of the Ford Motor Company. In the course of my stay there, I got to meet some interesting and important people, even being introduced to Henry Ford II on one occasion. It seems that even a small fish in a big pond can have fun if the members of the big pond are considerate and classy people. Ford's Christmas party that year was a fancy event at the Sherry Netherlands Hotel ballroom and the youngest employee from the mailroom (me) had too many cocktails. Being concerned that I get home in one piece, the office manager had me delivered home by a company chauffeur driven Lincoln. The following Monday when I reported to work everyone at Ford International knew Bob Brunelle. Fortunately we all had a good laugh. It seems I had gotten the Executive V.P.'s (Mr. Bogdan) ear and proceeded to tell him how to run the organization. (Mr. Bogdan's previous employment had been head financial advisor to General Douglas MacArthur in Japan.)

In September, 1951, I enrolled in City College of New York (CCNY) night school. In those years, CCNY did not charge tuition. My high school average had been on the order of 83% so it qualified me for entry. I did have to take a test but they advised me that this was merely a placement test. I continued working at Ford in the day and after work I would take a long subway ride uptown to 139th Street and Convent Avenue. CCNY was (and still is) a great Gothic edifice that looks more like a Gothic cathedral than a college.

By early 1952 the war in Korea was still raging and I began to become concerned that the army was about to draft me. (I had registered for the draft when I turned eighteen.) When I started considering my options, I decided to go to the Air Force recruitment office and see what they had to offer. Of course they presented the best "face forward" and told me of the various schools I could choose from so I decided to enlist. In February, 1952, they sent me to Whitehall Street in Manhattan for a physical which I passed, and then gave me a Basic Training start date of March 11, 1952. A very, very cold snowy winter day in early March, 1952 found me deposited at a God forsaken, wind blown basic training station in upstate New York. The name of the base was Sampson Air Force Base, the very place where, just a few years earlier, Brother Normand had spent a year at college. I imagine the abrupt end to Sampson College had been to convert the facility to an Air Force Basic Training base. Sampson had come full circle. From Navy base, to college, to Air Force base.

I will not burden the reader with reading about my personal agonies in basic training. The cold winds that blow in from Seneca Lake kept me deathly ill for almost the entire training. In addition to having "Pink Eye", I believe I had pneumonia but I refused to go to the hospital. This would have meant I would be put back to start all over again in a following group. Obviously I survived and got to choose my technical school which was the Army Engineer Drafting School at Ft. Belvoir, Virginia. Since the Air Force did not have a drafting school, they would temporarily assign their people to the Army for the duration of the school.

Normand and Connie

Around the time I went into the Air Force in 1952, my brother Normand had gotten a new draftsman job at an aircraft instrument company in Elmhurst, Queens. The name of the company was Kollsman Instrument Corporation and their main product line consisted of airplane altimeters, air speed indicators, turn and bank indicators and other related aviation devices. In 1950, two years before Normand left Sperry for Kollsman, my sister Connie had gotten a job at Sperry on Normand and Nancy's recommendation. Connie was to work in the same electrical assembly department as Nancy worked. Not to get ahead of the story, I will only say at this time that Connie was to continue working at Sperry for over nineteen years.

Bob – Air Force Service Continued – 1952

The Army Engineer Training Center at Ft. Belvoir, Virginia was and still is a huge military installation located about 25 miles southwest of Washington, D.C. I reported to Company A, 1st school battalion in early May. I was to spend the next three months or so struggling with the mysteries of triangles, straight edges and visual perception of objects with the intent of putting a drawing on paper. Never having had a drafting course in high school, I was at a disadvantage with other students who had. If one recalls the high school curriculums of the 1950s, those with academic curriculums like myself took college preparatory courses, not vocational type courses like drafting. Within a month or so, I was called into the Colonels office and advised that unless I got better grades, I was out. He did give me the option of going to night class as well as day to try and catch up. Fortunately going to night class pulled me out of my failing grades and I was able to graduate in early August 1952. My orders upon graduation gave me a month home leave after which I was to report to Camp Stoneman (San Francisco), California for subsequent shipment to duty in Korea.

CHAPTER **13**

My Military Service Years - 1952 to 1956

Passage to Korea

My flight from NYC to San Francisco was the second time I had flown. The first time was my flight from Sampson AFB to Washington DC in an Air Force chartered DC-3. The September 1952 flight from LaGuardia Airport, NY was a commercial flight in a four engine propeller airplane. I don't remember what type of airplane, possibly it was a Lockheed Constellation. As I write this account fifty-six years later (in 2008) I'm consciously aware of the progress aviation has made in the last half century. Leaving early in the morning and making numerous stops along the way, I was not to arrive in San Francisco until after 11:00 P.M California time. I recall being so exhausted that the annoyed stewardess had a hard time waking me up to apply my seat belt for landing. Grabbing a cab, I went to a hotel in San Francisco for the night and then took a bus to Camp Stoneman the next morning. I remained in Camp Stoneman for two weeks and went sightseeing in Frisco the next weekend. As people who know Frisco would recognize, the days in the summer are warm but the night can get quite cold. I didn't know whether to wear my khaki summer uniform or my blue wool winter uniform. Frisco is a beautiful city and unfortunately I have never been back there since 1952.

Finally the military sea transport people put me and more than a thousand other GIs, Army and Air Force, on a ship and we had an eleven day, somewhat uncomfortable trip to Yokahama, Japan. While on shipboard, I bumped into my best friend from high school days, Bill McGuire. We had a lot of fun talking over the "old days" which was of course just two years before. Bill was destined for a different Air Force base in Korea than myself. Upon arrival in Japan, we all (the Air Force types only) were put on a train and spent that night and half the next day traveling south through the Japanese countryside. We were being sent to an Australian AFB on the island of Kyushu for subsequent shipment by C-46 and C-47 flights to our individual Korean duty stations. When I awoke in the morning on the train (it was a sleeper), I raised my window shade to find a huge sun rising in the east; a beautiful sight. I now know why the rising sun is the symbol of Japan. One quick stop we made was at the railroad station in Hiroshima. Being only seven years after the dropping of the Atomic Bomb, signs of the explosion were still visible in the twisted steel girders of the industrial buildings along the rail line. I wondered what was on the minds of the Japanese people in the station as they saw a trainload of U.S. Air Force men going through their city.

K-13 Korea 1952 – 1953

The flight to Suwon, Korea (K-13) from Japan was a fairly short one. Upon landing, I went through base processing and was assigned to the 8th Air Installations Organization (8th AIO) which was a squadron of the 8th Fighter Bomber Wing (FBW). K-13 was the Air Force designation of the base near the town of Suwon. The next closest airbase was called Kimpo (K-14) which was located on the outskirts of Seoul.

The 8th FBW operated F-80 jet aircraft under three squadrons: the 35th FB Sq., the 36th FB Sq. and the 80th FB Sq. They had been in the Korean War from the very beginning, relocating a number of times in Korea as the tide of war moved up and down the Korean peninsula. Because of this fact, they had adopted the name "HOBOS" and it became our official call sign. Actually the 8th FBW had operated out of eight different airfields since the start of the war on 25 June 1950.

On 28 October 1952, a little over a month after I arrived at K-13, the 8th FBW celebrated the completion of its 50,000 combat sortie. Taking my camera to the flight line for the event, I got some good shots of the returning F-80 pulling up to a ceremony stage set up for the celebration. Over 50 years later I had occasion to see pictures of the event in an aviation magazine. It was a strange "Déjà vu" feeling.

Being in an air installation squadron made for a strange kind of war. You knew planes were occasionally being lost and men killed or missing, but you were not personally or specifically aware of the losses unless you were in a flying squadron. In December, just before Christmas 1952, an F-80 on a ferry flght mission struck a C-47 taxiing across the runway and all thirteen men in the transport and the F-80 pilot were killed. This event struck home with the entire base.

The duties of the 8th AIO were to help build and maintain all of the facilities of the airbase in conjunction with an Army engineering outfit which was located right outside the base perimeter. This Army outfit was called SCARWAF (Special Category Army with Air Force) and they maintained much of the heavy equipment (Bulldozers, road graders, etc.) which was needed for the mission. Many of the engineering people in SCARWAF had gone through the engineer school at Ft. Belvoir and one of my good Army friends (Jim Malloy) from my class had been separately shipped to Korea to this unit outside K-13.

Though we learned basic mechanical drafting, appropriately

the drafting curriculum at Ft. Belvoir had been heavily geared toward civil engineering and architectural drafting. My duties in AIO Engineering required all of these skills. In addition to making working drawings for new base buildings, we also were making a map of the base on a scale of one inch equals 200 feet. Having been built quickly and with minimum planning, no comprehensive map existed. The engineering staff consisted of myself and two other draftsmen, an elderly civilian Korean engineer, an Air Force surveyor (Sergeant Ted Turnley) and two Korean civilian surveyors. A staff sergeant was in charge of the entire office and he reported to a young second lieutenant who had arrived shortly after myself and was a graduate of the Virginia Military Institute (VMI).

Our office was a standard tropical shell building with no insulation, built of wood studs and corrugated metal exterior. The reader need only envision the TV series "MASH" to picture what the building looked like. We had a large cast iron pot bellied stove in the center of the drafting area to keep us warm in the extremely cold Korean winter. We worked seven day weeks and took time out Sunday morning to attend religious services if we wished. During my tour in Korea (twelve months), we designed and built a new base chapel. Rushing to get the chapel built before Christmas 1952, we were rewarded with the presence of Cardinal Spellman (the military Vicar) saying Christmas midnight mass. As we shook his hand upon leaving the chapel, he had us sign our names and outfit in a book in the rear of the church. A couple of months later, my Mom received a letter from the Cardinal saying he had met her son at Christmas and all was well.

Our living quarters were fairly comfortable given that we were in Korea. The AIO squadron was housed in a half dozen small metal corrugated Quonset huts which were heated by two pot bellied stoves, one at each end of the huts. Our beds were wood and canvas folding cots and our mattress (self bought) were air mattresses. Our bathrooms were outdoor "outhouses" and our washroom was a tent set up with showers. One luxury we had was a "house boy" that we hired (as a group) to keep the hut clean, make our beds and do other chores. There were many poor Korean children, some orphans, and this arrangement helped them greatly. It was a mutually beneficial arrangement. Our commanding officer, who was a major, was housed in his own Quonset hut with the two other officers from the squadron.

Our "chow hall" was a large tropical shell building which served the entire 8th FBW. Usually in the evening hours after work and chow we would go to another large tropical shell building that served as an Airmen's Club. I believe the beer was 25 cents a bottle. Being nineteen years old at the time, I could drink in the service but not in many states in the U.S. No hard alcohol (whiskey) was served to the enlisted men. This was reserved for the officers and was served at their own "Officers Club". It always amazed me that men who were flying combat missions constantly consumed so much alcohol.

Though we worked seven day weeks, we did get a Rest and Recuperation (R&R) week off in Japan every three months if we so wished. We would fly from our base by military aircraft (of course) to the city in Japan that we had selected for the R&R. (There was a selection of about three cities you could choose from.)

The duty was pretty routine and it got somewhat boring given the seven day weeks. About the only excitement was an occasional "Bed Check Charlie" night raid by slow, propeller driven North Korean aircraft that invariably occasioned the firing of our Army anti-aircraft guns. The base was wisely ringed with half track vehicles that mounted quad 50 caliber machine guns. The Army personnel lived in tents lined with plywood interiors that were set up next to their guns.

The storage fuel tanks for our jet aircraft (JP4 fuel) were located on the eastern perimeter of the base and were some concern to the base brass. Fearing that a "Bed Check Charlie" might score a lucky hit on a storage tank in a night raid, the AIO was given the assignment of surveying a site in the hills south of the base for a new and safer fuel tank location.

Consequently in the winter of 1952 – 1953, Sgt. Ted Turnley and his Korean surveyors would load up their levels, transits, rods, etc. every day in a ¾ ton weapons carrier and proceed to the hills south of the base to survey a new location for the jet fuel tanks. By winter I was getting cabin fever in my drafting room and prevailed on Turnley to allow me to tag along with the surveying team. From this time until I rotated back to the states in August 1953, I was to spend more time surveying than drafting. The winter months in the hills south of the base were extremely cold but it was worth it to get out in the field.

In the spring of 1953 we were given an assignment to survey locations for a white stripe to be painted down the center of the 9,000 foot long by 200 foot wide runway. Jet aircraft usually took off on combat missions side by side (one slightly ahead of the other) leaving from the south end of the runway and taking off at the north end. The white line down the center would help guide the pilots to stay on their side of the runway as they took off. Since the runway was operational throughout the daylight hours, we had to perform our survey on a "hot" runway. We had made arrangements with the tower to flash us a red warning light when a plane was preparing to take off or land. The arrangement worked fine for a while, however, on our second day on the runway, we found ourselves nearly run over by a couple of F-94 jets which came at us from the north end of the runway. Turnley, being the dedicated surveyor, grabbed his transit and hit the deck. Fortunately the F-94s took off with their powerful afterburners on and they were sufficiently airborne to clear us. We apparently had missed the tower warning and also had not figured on jets taking off "with the wind" from the north end. The F-94 was the Air Force's first jet radar night fighter and their squadron, being located at the runway's north end, could conveniently take off from that end using their additional power.

One other incident worth mentioning during my surveying

days concerns my encounter with a famous Tuskegee Airman. On a warm summer day in 1953, Turnley asked me to lead the surveying team to the other side of the base to continue to take measurements for the new base map we were making. Since the team consisted of only Koreans, with the exception of Turnley and myself, if Turnley couldn't lead the team, I would have to. Koreans were not allowed to be anywhere on the base unless accompanied by a G.I. The other side of the base was occupied by F-86 fighter jets of the famous 51st Fighter Interceptor Wing. While my wing flew older, slower F-80 fighter bombers, the F-86 wing were the guys who were daily doing battle with the enemy MIG-15 aircraft around the border of North Korea and China. While we were surveying in waist high grass west of the 51st FBW housing, a jeep rapidly approached us. The next thing I knew, a "black" full bird Colonel dressed in fatigues and wearing a pearl handle pistol was politely inquiring what we were doing. Quickly recovering from my surprise and forgetting to salute, I explained who we were and described what we were doing. Satisfied, the Colonel said we could "carry on", jumped in his jeep and departed. Upon returning to Engineering, I told my sergeant what had happened and inquired who the Colonel was. It seems his name was Benjamin O. Davis Jr. and he was the new commanding officer of the 51st Wing. I later found out more about Colonel Davis and continued to follow his career over the years. He had been the only black to graduate from West Point in the 20th century (until the 1950's), commanded the black 332nd Fighter Group (Tuskegee Airmen) in World War II and eventually he retired as a three-star general. General Davis died in 2002 at the age of 89.

While I am dropping famous names, I should mention two other notable men who crossed my path at K-13 though I did not personally meet either of them. During the winter of 1952-53 Ted Williams, the baseball player and Marine Corps pilot crashed landed his plane on our runway. I did not see it happen but a friend did and described to me that Williams landed his damaged Panther jet "wheels up" on the dirt adjacent to the runway. Immediately upon stopping, he popped his canopy and ran. We joked at the time that he had probably broken his baseball base running speed record on that occasion.

The other notable airman to fly at K-13 was Marine Corps pilot John Glenn. The last month of the war Glenn was an exchange pilot on loan to the Air Force and flew an F-86 fighter for the 51st Fighter Interceptor Wing. He shot down three MIGs in his short tour. Of course none of us knew anything about him in Korea since this was long before he became famous.

In early spring 1953, the 8th FBW began to transition from F-80 aircraft to the new F-86 Sabre jet. Our mission remained the same; we were still a fighter bomber wing. By summer all of the 8th's planes were Sabres. An armistice agreement with North Korea was signed on July 27, 1953 and a cease fire went into effect. The war was finally over. Coincidentally, my tour of duty was also at an end.

My orders dated 5 August 1953 assigned me to the 507th Tactical Control Group at Pope Air Force Base, Fort Bragg, North Carolina. I was given thirteen days travel time (in the U.S.) which would allow me a few days home leave time. I flew back to Japan and waited about a week before I was put on the USNS ship Darby which docked in Seattle, Washington in late August. Surprisingly, I was processed the same day I arrived and quickly caught a commercial airline back to New York City.

North Carolina 1953 – 1954

Pope AFB was a troop carrier base located on the huge Fort Bragg reservation which was (and still is) the home of the Army 82nd Airborne Division. The planes used in this period were mainly C-119 and C-124 troop carrier aircraft. Upon arrival I was assigned to the 728th Aircraft Control & Warning Squadron which was a unit of the 507th Group. My outfit was a mobile radar squadron which operated as a unit of the Tactical Control Group. That is, we were not static radar for the Pope AFB, rather we were mobile and had the capability to be moved from one location to another as the tactical situation dictated. All of our radar and communication equipment was mounted on trucks and trailers. We had our own mobile chow hall and cooks as well as motor pool, etc. Essentially, we could be self sufficient and motor our outfit and set up radar at different locations. When the move was too far for motoring, the Air Force would load our entire squadron: trucks, radar, men, etc. on C-124 aircraft and fly us to the closest Air Force base to the area of operations. When the Army airborne went on maneuvers in the field on Fort Bragg, we also went to the field and lived in eight men tents for the duration of maneuvers.

My job in the squadron was termed a draftsman position, however, it wasn't a civil engineering drafting position as I held in Korea. It was mainly a somewhat boring drafting of maps and map overlays that were used in the plotting of aircraft positions that represented aircraft that were picked up by our search radar. Individual aircraft plots were located and recorded on map overlays for a specific period of time and sent every month to higher headquarters. The overlays were called "Spotted Dogs".

South Carolina 1954 - 1956

In the spring of 1954, the 728th Aircraft Control & Warning Squadron was moved lock, stock and barrel to Donaldson AFB at Greenville, South Carolina. Donaldson was mainly a troop carrier wing for Army Airborne and our outfit's function remained basically the same as it had been at Fort Bragg. As a matter of fact, when the 82nd Airborne went on maneuvers on Fort Bragg, we would load our entire outfit on C-124's and fly back to live in the field in North Carolina. When maneuvers were over, back we would fly to our home in Greenville.

It seems that every squadron has a professional student and being utterly bored with my work, I volunteered for select schools that would take me to various bases in the U.S. In the fall of 1954, I volunteered for an A.F. school at Langley AFB in Virginia that taught NCOs the basics of Nuclear, Chemical and Biological warfare. By this time I had gained Sergeant's stripes and qualified as an NCO (Non Commissioned Officer). I had purchased a brand new 1954 Ford earlier in the year and packed my bags and drove to Virginia. After spending three months at Langley, I returned to my permanent station in Greenville.

In the spring of 1955, I was able to get sent to a school at Lowry AFB in Denver, Colorado that taught a more advanced Nuclear, Chemical and Biological course. Again I jumped into my trusted 1954 Ford and had a leisurely trip cross country to Denver. This course was also a three month course and on my weekends off I enjoyed the sights in Colorado's Rocky Mountains.

Returning to South Carolina in September of 1955, I began to make plans for my eventual and long anticipated separation from the Air Force. My scheduled separation date was March 10, 1956, however, I became aware that there was an early release program that allowed airmen to get out early to attend college. Being unable to get myself back into City College of N.Y. (CCNY) in time for the January, 1956 semester, I was able to enroll at Clemson A&M College in Clemson, South Carolina. Per orders dated 28 December 1955, I was released from the Air Force effective 21 January 1956.

In late January 1956, I drove approximately 40 miles south from Donaldson AFB to Clemson, South Carolina. Clemson was at this time an Agricultural and Mechanical College that had courses ranging from Animal Husbandry to Electrical, Mechanical and Civil Engineering. I enrolled as a freshman in the civil engineering curriculum and proceeded to re-enter an academic environment. Though adjustment from a military environment to an academic life was initially difficult, within a few weeks my complete concentration on my studies unconsciously "nudged" me comfortably into my new life. After taking my semester final exams in May, I was pleasantly surprised to find I had averaged better than "B" in my courses.

CHAPTER **14**

Life in the Long Island City House - 1950 to 1970

Connie Gil 1950 - 1970

As previously stated in Chapter Twelve, my sister Connie (Brunelle) Gil had (in 1950) obtained a job at Sperry Gyroscope Corporation in Great Neck Long Island. At the time of her employment, both brother Normand and his soon to be wife Nancy Mattson also worked at Sperry. Connie was to work at Sperry for nineteen years, finally leaving in 1969. During that time she was to occupy a number of positions in the Electrical Assembly Department.

In the years after her marriage to Tom Gil and until 1959 Connie and Tom lived in a number of apartments in Queens, N.Y.C. In the aftermath of WWII, housing was almost impossible to obtain in New York and what was available was expensive and often substandard. Although Mom and Dad owned the three apartment brownstone in Long Island City in that period, because of Rent Control Regulations they could not obtain an apartment for Connie in their own house. The first floor apartment was occupied by two elderly gentlemen, the second floor by an elderly married couple (Mr. & Mrs. Charles Schaefer) and Mom and Dad occupied the third (top) floor.

Finally in 1959, the first floor became available (both gentlemen had died) and Connie and Tom moved in. By the early 1950's, Tom had left the Fisher Baking Company and purchased a gasoline and car repair Shell station in Astoria, NY with his brother-in-law (his sister's husband Frank Ricco). Connie and Tom each had their own cars and Connie would drive to work going east on the newly constructed Long Island Expressway (LIE), (later derisively called the "Long Island Distressway") and Tom making a short trip to Astoria (next to L.I.C.). Not having children, they continued to live like newlyweds, engaging in various pursuits such as skiing in New England and Canada and vacations to Cuba, etc.

In 1970, Connie obtained a job in the Social Services Dept. of the City of New York. By this point in her life she was now single, having divorced from Tom Gil in 1964. After their divorce, Connie continued to live in the L. I. C. house on 45th Ave. Tom obtained an apartment in Sunnyside, Queens. He subsequently remarried, built a lakefront house in Lake Montauk on Long Island and went to work for the U.S. Postal Service.

Connie was to work for the City of N.Y. Social Services for eighteen years and in 1988 decided to retire at the age of sixty two. Mother had prevailed on her to retire early, though Connie says she was at the time inclined to work until she reached sixty-five.

The House Gets Rebuilt 1956 - 1957

In 1956 Uncle Gene and Aunt Bea sold their half of the property in L.I.C. to Mom and Dad. Gene and Bea had bought a one family house in New Hyde Park, L.I. and then moved from their apartment on Flatbush Avenue, Brooklyn. Dad again proceeded to make major improvements on the house that he and Mom had previously wanted to make but were reluctant to ask Uncle Gene to go along with. A new gas heating furnace for central heating, new brass plumbing for the entire house, a new kitchen for the third floor apartment, new bathrooms for all three apartments and many more improvements were made. Their next door neighbor at the time was a fine cabinetmaker who worked in townhouses in Manhattan and the folks hired him to make all the new cabinets in the kitchen, major woodwork in the dining room (cabinets, paneling) and paneling in the living room. The cabinetmaker was a German immigrant named Bill who spoke English with a heavy German accent. He and Mom developed a good working relationship and Mom used to call him "Der Bill" in a German accent.

"Der Bill'

After building the new kitchen, Mom had gained considerable confidence in "Der Bill" and she proceeded to rebuild her living room and dining room per "Der Bill's" suggestion. This involved tearing down half the walls between the kitchen and the living room and between the living room and the dining room. Dad almost had a heart attack when he came home from work one day and found three rooms of his house in shambles. Plaster and slats were all over the floor and only bare wood vertical beams were between the rooms holding up three ceilings. "Der Bill" stood amid the carnage, his head surrounded by plaster dust.

I am happy to report that "Der Bill" did a beautiful job rebuilding and opening up the rooms, blending together various woods (mahogany, cherry, pine, etc.) into beautiful cabinets and paneling. For years later, Mom insisted on standing in front of her renovated rooms when photos were taken of her. All is well that ends well we used to tell Dad of the experience.

Bob Brunelle 1956 – 1959

After my spring semester at Clemson in 1956, I returned home to my old boyhood room in the L.I.C. house and reregistered as a second semester freshman at City College of NY (CCNY). I was to spend the next two and a half years at CCNY until in 1958 brother Normand said he would get me a job interview at Kollsman Instrument Corp (KIC) in Elmhurst, Queens. By this time Normand had been working at KIC for eight years and had worked his way up from a draftsman position to a Product Engineer position. I went to the job interview and was hired as a draftsman by the Chief Draftsman, Sal Martucci. The Drafting Department was fairly large and consisted of possibly thirty draftsman and designers. Having had a draftsman position in the Air Force and drafting courses in college had given me a good entry to the interview.

In 1958 I withdrew from CCNY in good standing. My decision to leave college was a difficult one in that my grades were passing but just average. I was now dating a girl named Barbara Wann from Sunnyside, Queens who I had met while in the service a few years previously on a train trip from South Carolina to N.Y.C. By 1959 I was 26 years old and felt I should get on with my life. On June 4, 1959 we were married in a Baptist church in Sunnyside, Queens and moved into a three room apartment in Jackson Heights, Queens, adjacent to LaGuardia Airport.

CHAPTER **15**

A Decade of Personal Change   1959 – 1968

New York   1959 – 1962

My early married life with Barbara was fairly ordinary for a newlywed couple. Our apartment in Jackson Heights was only a ten minute drive from home to my work and Barbara had taken a new job as a representative with the New York Telephone Company, also located in Queens. My fairly new position with KIC was going well and I was learning a lot about aircraft instruments and how to make drawings of them for manufacturing by the machine shop, optical shop and assembly departments.

We decided to give ourselves a year or more to get adjusted to married life before having children. In the spring of 1960 Barbara became pregnant and our daughter Katherine Lynn Brunelle was born at Flushing Hospital, Queens on January 30, 1961. The day after Katherine was born, we had a huge snowstorm in N.Y.C. The snow was so deep that Mayor John Lindsay completely banned civilian traffic on the city streets in order to allow snow clearance by the Dept. of Sanitation. Unfortunately the snow removal went badly and the auto ban lasted over a week. In the meantime, people were still being admitted to the hospitals and when space became exhausted, patients were being bedded in the hospital halls. Though maternity stays were a few days long in the 1960s, after six days the police were authorized to bring home patients in police cars.

On the seventh day of Barbara's maternity stay, Connie's husband Tom volunteered to go fetch Barbara and baby Katherine in the tow truck of his Shell service station. Tom and I fetched our delicate baggage and drove home to L.I.C. We were unable to get through to our apartment in Jackson Heights because the street (93rd St.) was not yet plowed. Consequently, daughter Kathy spent the second week of her life in her grandparents house in L.I.C. The people of N.Y.C. took their and my final revenge on Mayor Lindsay by voting him out of office the next election.

By late 1961 I was promoted to a position of Senior Draftsman with a corresponding increase in salary. The salary increase was surely welcome but what happened in 1961 was even more welcome. President Kennedy's commitment to go to the moon in the decade of the 60s had begun to resonate with the aerospace industry and the reputation of KIC was already prominent in the aviation industry. Of particular importance was the fact that KIC had for a number of years been making a navigational sextant for the Boeing B-52 bomber. Based on this fact and a successful proposal and bid for a sextant to be used on the Apollo spacecraft, KIC in early 1962 received an initial contract for 42 million dollars from the National Aeronautics and Space Administration (NASA) to design and manufacture an automatic sextant.

The sextant was to be designed by KIC people working at and with the guidance of the Massachusetts Institute of Technology Instrumentation Laboratory (MITIL) in Cambridge, Mass. The plan was to have our people design and generate the working drawings in Cambridge and send the drawings to the KIC facility in Syosset, L.I. for manufacture.

Accordingly, KIC management recruited and selected an initial team of ten engineers, designers and draftsmen to relocate to the

Boston area to perform on the contract at MITIL. For myself, the promotion to Senior Draftsman had been just in time since the company was selecting only "Senior" positions. Six months earlier I could not have applied for the position. Mr. Martucci, the chief of drafting advised me I could have one of the slots if I wanted it so Barbara and I talked and thought it over, weighing the pros and cons of moving to Boston.

It turned out the pros outweighed the cons. Working at MIT would be a great experience career wise. In addition to the job experience it would certainly look good on a resume. In housing terms, it would not be to disruptive and would certainly be financially profitable. The company would pay for my housing costs in Boston. Since we were renting in N.Y.C. we could rent an apartment in Boston at no expense to ourselves and give up the N.Y.C. apartment. In terms of schooling, daughter Katherine was only a year and a half old, therefore, we had no school transfer issues. In terms of Barbara's job, she had not yet gone back to work since Kathy was born. In terms of my salary, it would remain the same but the company would have me on an expense account which would almost double my salary. In terms of returning to N.Y.C. to visit relatives, etc., the company was willing to pay my traveling expenses for a trip every other weekend if I wished. I won't list the cons we discussed but clearly the pros won out.

Boston 1962 – 1965

In August of 1962 Barbara and I took a trip to Boston and found a beautiful apartment on Commonwealth Avenue in an upscale section of the city. We then packed and moved all our possessions, furniture, etc. to the new apartment. Contrary to my expectations, my new work facility was a very old concrete loft building on Albany Street in an industrial area of Cambridge. At this time MITIL (the Lab) had two facilities; this one and a more modern building on Cambridge Parkway adjacent to the Charles

River. The director of "The Lab" was a 61 year old gentlemen named Charles Stark Draper. Though Dr. Draper's name may not be known to the average citizen, he was well known in the field of air and space navigation. He is in fact known as the "Father of Inertial Navigation" and its theory and development was a result of Dr. Draper's genius and efforts. My immediate boss was a KIC engineer named Thornton Stearns and my MIT group leader was a gentlemen named Phil Bowditch.

The first few months of the job proved to be uneventful. The designers in the group began making layouts of the instrument that MIT had previously conceived and we draftsmen would refer to the layouts and generate working drawings.

After about four months of slow effort, Phil Bowditch came in one day and said "Stop all work." It seems that "The Lab" people had a change of heart concerning the basic design configuration and we had to scrap all our designs and drawings. We then started from scratch with a new design concept. I am writing about this episode forty years after the successful landing on the moon by the U.S., therefore, a loss of four months doesn't seem significant. Quite a different view was held in early 1963. One might forget that at this time the U.S. was in a desperate space race with Russia and it was anyone's guess who would win.

Before we were to begin again with a new design, our entire group was moved to the other Lab building on Cambridge Parkway. This facility proved to be a much more pleasant and scenic location and I feel it greatly contributed to our renewed design efforts. The work environment was professional but very informal and relaxed. It was an academic environment actually. Phil Bowditch set the pace. In the summer, he would stroll into the office at 9:30 A.M., cigarette in hand and wearing bermuda shorts, thereby setting the dress code for all. He would then have his coffee in hand and make the rounds to our drawing boards around 10:00 A.M.. At Christmas time the Lab had a huge party for the employees and spouses at the Lab's expense. Dr. Draper presided at the party, having a great time eating, drinking and contributing humorous stories and jokes.

In 1963 four astronauts paid us a visit and I got to see John Glenn whose path had crossed mine in Korea exactly a decade earlier. Before leaving, they presented Dr. Draper a short handwritten and individually signed note on MIT letterhead which read as follows:

> *With all good wishes for success to the builders of the system from the users of the hardware."*
>
> *Alan B. Shepard Jr.*
> *M. Scott Carpenter*
> *J. H. Glenn Jr.*
> *D. K. Slayton*

Dr. Draper had another illustrious but more private visitor on a subsequent occasion. One morning (in 1964 I believe) I went up to the third floor of the Lab to take some measurements from a full size wooden mockup of the navigational section of the Apollo Spacecraft. The mockup stood alone in the center of a large otherwise empty room. As I entered the room I observed Dr. Draper talking to a short, elderly gentlemen and they were examining and talking about the mockup. I immediately turned around and exited the area, not wanting to disturb Dr. Draper. When lunch time arrived I encountered both men again as they were exiting the building, apparently going to lunch. The two men got into Dr. Draper's old Buick auto and drove off. It was then that I recognized the other man. It was Jimmy Doolittle. The thought occurred to me that any police officer or other citizen observing the two short, elderly men in Draper's old Buick would never recognize that the car contained two of the most famous aviation pioneers in history.

In the spring of 1964 Barbara and I bought a new Oldsmobile Cutlass automobile. We traded in my year old 1963 Cutlass because I no longer trusted its safety. On one of our many trips between Boston and N.Y.C. we had an accident which I believed was due to faulty brakes. Since the '64 Cutlass was an entirely new design, I though it unlikely that GM had carried over the brake fault.

Taking my vacation in July '64 we went to Martinsville, Virginia to vacation and visit Barbara's grandmother. Though Barbara's mother now lived in N.Y.C., Barbara had grown up and gone to school in Martinsville. When we returned to Boston, Barbara advised me that she was very unhappy living in Boston and for that matter no longer wanted to live in N.Y. In early fall 1964 Barbara visited with her mother in N.Y.C. and then left with our daughter Kathy from there to live at her grandmother's home in Virginia. Months of bitter legal dispute began and agreement between ourselves was only reached when custody of Kathy and visitation rights were established. Since Barbara insisted on living in Virginia, I was to have Kathy stay with me during Christmas and Easter vacations, and for at least two months in the summer. I would pay Barbara child support for the time Kathy was in Virginia. The divorce became final in early 1965. Kathy came to live with me in Boston for a couple of months in early 1965 at which time my aunt Regina Villeneuve in nearby Rhode Island acted as babysitter. Kathy returned to live with me in the summer of 1965 and I enrolled her in a nursery school in Boston. I would leave her off on my way to work and would pick her up on my way home from the Lab.

By the summer of 1965 our work at MIT was ending. All the design and drafting had been completed as per the NASA contract requirements with KIC. The sextant parts were being manufactured at the KIC facilities in New York. The mechanical parts were being manufactured at the KIC Space Division in Syosset, Long Island and the optical components were being manufactured at the KIC Optical Division in Elmhurst, Queens, New York. Of course when the contract was complete all we Kollsman (KIC) people were able to return to our previous KIC positions in New York. MIT demonstrated to all of us that they were very happy with the work we had done and said they would entertain any job applications from those of us who wished to remain at MIT. Two draftsmen and two designers chose to remain in Boston and all but one of these were hired by the Lab.

Epilogue to MITIL

The late 1960s and the Vietnam period produced a rash of protests by college students to associations between college research labs and the Federal Government. In the early 1970s, MIT was forced to divest itself of the Lab. The Lab and its staff remained in existence in the Cambridge area with much the same staff. In deference to Dr. Draper (who had started the Lab during WW II) the new company was called "The Charles Stark Draper Laboratory Inc". The Lab continues to do state-of-the-art research and development for the U.S. military, NASA and other government agencies.

Back to New York 1965 – 1969

In October 1965, I returned to New York and moved back into my boyhood bedroom in Mom and Dad's apartment in the Long Island City brownstone. I was now single and daughter Kathy was living with her mother in Virginia. I resumed my job at the Kollsman (KIC) facility in Syosset, Long Island. Syosset was approximately 27 miles by car on the Long Island "Distressway" from L.I.C. I was reassigned to the Space Division and again put on the Apollo Program which was continuing at the Syosset facility.

Though design of the sextant contract had been fully completed at MITIL, Kollsman had subsequently received a NASA contract for an Alignment Optical Telescope (AOT) to be used and mounted in the Lunar Excursion Module (LEM). (The sextant was mounted in the Command Module.) The design of this telescope had been almost completed at MITIL, however, some design refinements remained to be accomplished.

The LEM group was a rather small group which consisted of one engineer (Walter Chin), one designer (myself) and one optical engineer (Bob Pitlak). We did not have a dedicated draftsman and if we could not get a draftsman when we needed one, I would perform this function as well. Shortly after returning to New York I had been promoted to Senior Designer position. We all reported to a chief engineer named John Fabbroni.

The mid to late 1960s in the space race era were exciting years. We were running out of time in terms of beating the Russians to the moon and the entire space program ran into serious difficulties on the 27th of January 1967. On that date, three Apollo astronauts were killed in a fire during ground command module tests at Cape Kennedy. All of a sudden the space program experienced a complete paradigm shift for NASA as well as a disastrous loss of scheduled time. Subcontractors such as KIC were directed to completely re-examine the designs, particularly as they related to crew safety. My small group found itself working long hours and six day weeks. On a couple of occasions I worked seven day weeks.

When I returned to New York in 1965 I found that I had to completely reconstruct my personal and social life. This was not an easy task since I had been married for the last five years and I found it difficult to be a bachelor again. Added to this was that when daughter Kathy came to stay with me during holidays and summer months, I was no longer a bachelor but a single father. I had decided not to stay in Boston for this reason. Living in the Long Island City house I was able to receive some assistance from

Mom and Dad. I did go out on dates occasionally, however, in early 1967 I met a girl who worked at KIC (the secretary to the Environmental Dept. chief) who I became very fond of. Her name was Marta Babb and we dated exclusively until April 28, 1968 when we were married in a Greek Orthodox church on Long Island.

1968 Assassinations, Riots, Revolution and Space Travel

In late 1966 the second floor tenants in Mom and Dad's house retired to Florida and their apartment became available to me. I proceeded to renovate the apartment (painting, etc.) for my eventual move. When Marta and I decided to get married, we both began working on the apartment. By the time we married, it was ready to move in. In hindsight, the entire year of 1968 was a blur to me as I suspect it was to the entire nation. I was very busy at work and still involved with the space program as well as working with Marta to finish the apartment. Marta was very busy finalizing and making plans for our wedding in April. There were church preparations as well as invitations, reception plans, etc. to be completed.

We were so occupied that we were barely aware of all the world-shaking events that were taking place. On the 31st of January 1968, the Vietcong launched the huge Tet Offensive in Vietnam. Each night when we watched the news at supper, we witnessed the carnage and deaths on the television screen. We now had almost half a million soldiers in Vietnam. On April 4, less than a month before our wedding, Martin Luther King was shot dead in Memphis, Tennessee. Riots, looting and burning followed shortly thereafter in many American cities. On June 5th, three days before my 35th birthday, Robert Kennedy was shot and killed in Los Angeles following his victory in the California presidential primary election. On August 21 and 22, Soviet forces invaded Czechoslovakia to restore strict Communism to that country.

Finally some good news. On the 21st of December, U.S. astronauts Lovell, Anders and Borman completed the first flight around the Moon in Apollo 8. After having been intimately involved in the Apollo program for the last eight years, I was emotionally moved when an Apollo 8 astronaut quoted from Genesis on Christmas Eve: "In the beginning God created the heavens and the earth. Now the Earth proved to be formless and waste and there was darkness upon the surface......". To me, the Genesis reading seemed to signify that our efforts had been ordained by God. With the exception of our marriage, the year was full of turmoil. Finally great news had closed out 1968. Successful flights of Apollo 9 and 10 followed, further checking out the Apollo equipment. The final triumph came on July 20, 1969 with the landing of Apollo 11 on the moon's surface. John F. Kennedy's commitment to land on the moon in the decade of the 60s had been fulfilled. More than 300,000 American workers and 20,000 companies had contributed to the national mission.

CHAPTER **16**

From the Author's Perspective 1970 – 1997

As previously stated, my sister Connie had retired from work in 1970. Mom and Dad had retired in 1964 when the textile company they worked for (Geffen Textiles) went out of business. Being an active man, Dad continued to find pleasure in working on the house, painting, fixing things, etc. Both of them began making more visits to surviving relatives in Rhode Island. They even took a train trip to Florida to visit good friends from their church that had moved there. Mom would not fly. Though she had been born six months before the Wright Brothers made their first flight, she never trusted airplanes. As an elderly lady, whenever she was asked what she thought contributed to her longevity, she would humorously say "staying out of airplanes". I wonder if she ever thought about the fact that both of her sons were spending the majority of their working careers in the aviation industry and that both had been in the U. S. Air Force.

1970 - 1973

By 1970 all of the Brunelle family with the exception of Normand's family were living in the house in Long Island City. Connie was living in the first floor apartment, Marta and I on the second floor and Mom and Dad on the third floor. Normand was living in the house he and Nancy had bought in Glen Cove, Long Island in 1955. By this time Normand and Nancy had four children: Anders born December 21, 1956, Guy born April 16, 1958, Kyle born January 7, 1960 and Christiane born January 26, 1965. Marta and I had our first child, a girl we named Lesley on October 22, 1970. Both Normand and I were still working at KIC in Syosset, Long Island. Marta had left KIC in early 1969 and obtained a secretarial position locally in Long Island City until she became pregnant with Lesley. When Lesley was around two and a half, Marta returned to work and Mom took care of Lesley for about a year.

Father's Illness 1974 - 1975

In the summer of 1974, Mom, Dad and Connie made a trip to Rhode Island to visit relatives. When they returned, Connie advised me that on the return trip, Dad had a minor fender bender accident which had no damage to the other car and only slight damage to Dad's. She told me this in confidence because she didn't want to offend Dad. She had also noticed that throughout the trip Dad did not seem to be driving very well. Mom added that Dad had of late been forgetting little things and had been complaining that noises such as closing of doors in the building hallway was disturbing him. Within a few weeks, Mom and Connie began to notice that Dad's forgetfulness of ordinary things was getting worse.

Mom persuaded Dad that they should go to the family doctor (Dr. Wilner) to get a checkup. After examining Dad, the doctor told them that he could find nothing wrong and that perhaps Dad was beginning mild dementia. Dad was 73 years old at this time. Within a short period of time, Dad's forgetfulness began getting worse. A nurse friend of Mom's advised her that they should consult a neurologist. Their visit to the neurologist produced disturbing news. The doctor suspected a brain tumor and sent Dad for further tests. Further tests performed at St. Barnabas Hospital in the Bronx confirmed the diagnosis; Dad did have a brain tumor.

The chief brain surgeon at St. Barnabus Hospital was a very famous doctor named Irving S. Cooper who had pioneered in surgery for all types of neurological illness. After examining Dad's test, he consulted with Mom, Connie and Normand. His conclusion and recommendation – Dad's tumor was non-operable. If an operation were to be performed, they could not get all of the tumor and possibly Dad would lose control of various parts of his body. He put it to them this way: "If it was my father, I would let the illness take its course." He would give Dad medications to reduce the swelling and pressure in the brain. He estimated that Dad had about a year to live.

Dad returned home. The family decided to take Dr. Cooper's advice. Mom and Connie took care of Dad, alternating night duty when Dad began to get worse. We never told Dad that he had a brain tumor and he never asked. In the early months of his illness I believe he knew what his problem was. Many days he would put on his work clothes and go about his house chores. He would paint, fix door knobs, sweep the sidewalk, do minor cement work in the back yard and did not appear to be in any pain. As the illness progressed, they gave Dad increasing doses of medicine. One night at the end of October 1975, Connie sat up all night with Dad and told us that on a couple of occasions she thought he was dying. Dad returned to St. Barnabas November 2nd, 1975 and died in the afternoon of November 8th. His body was cremated the morning of November 11, 1975, Armistice Day.

Christopher Brunelle - 1974

Our second child Christopher Brunelle was born March 14, 1974. Marta and I could not agree on a name, therefore, we compromised. If Christopher was born on March 17 we would name him Patrick (for St. Patrick's Day). Otherwise we would name him Christopher James, Marta's choice. Mind you, this is <u>before</u> the time doctors could tell the sex of your child before birth. We never agreed on a girl's name. It is fortunate that we had a boy.

Normand and Bob Return to College 1972 - 1975

In 1972 my brother Normand decided to return to college and get his degree. He had left Brooklyn Polytechnic Institute in his third year when he ran out of GI Bill assistance. Rather than go for a degree in Engineering, he switched his major to Business Administration and registered for C. W. Post College of Long Island University in Greenvale, Long Island. The college is located a few miles from Normand's house in Glen Cove, therefore, it was very convenient. He would go to classes in the evening after work at KIC and then drive the five or so miles home. Normand completed his degree in May of 1974. He was at this time forty-eight years old.

In 1973, I decided to return to college also. A cousin of mine, Ben Tellier, had mentioned to me that the Korean War GI Bill benefits had not yet expired, though it was twenty years since the war. When I inquired, I found this was true and that on the basis of my nearly four years in the Air Force, I still had over two years of benefits to collect. Since I was working at KIC with Normand, I also found it convenient to go to C. W. Post College. Like Normand I decided to change my major. Having always enjoyed history, I decided to major in history and political science. The college accepted over two years of transfer credits from my previous colleges and taking a heavy credit load at night I was able to get my degree in January 1975. I was at this time forty two years old.

One may ask why two guys in their forties would decide to go back to college, particularly since both of us had obviously done fairly well in our careers without degrees. I believe the answer for

both of us may be threefold as follows:
1. The desire to finish a goal we had started but not completed.
2. The subconscious feeling of career insecurity knowing we were in middle age without degrees.
3. The feeling that it was time to change careers and that we had better diversify our knowledge and education.

Kollsman Instrument Corporation (KIC) - 1975

As fate would have it, our decisions came just in time for career and employment moves. In the early 1970s, KIC was bought by a company called Sun Chemical. By 1973 rumors began circulating that Sun Chemical planned to move KIC out of state. Beginning in 1969 with the ending of the Apollo program, the company had laid off much of its engineering staff. This of course is not unusual in the aerospace industry. Jobs come and go with contracts. Normand and I had been lucky to survive as long as we had. By 1975 Normand had been with KIC for twenty-five years and I for seventeen years.

By the end of 1975 KIC moved "lock, stock and barrel" to Nashua, New Hampshire (NH). Out of almost 2,000 employees, only about 400 had moved with KIC to NH. Over 1,500 employees (engineers, machinists, assembly people, administrative types, etc.) found themselves without jobs by December 1975. The real difficulty was that "fate" had dealt us a "double whammy". The year 1975 was a terrible year for the U.S. economy and high tech (or any) jobs on Long Island and the rest of the country were impossible to find.

The 1975 – 1976 "Recession"

As I write the above heading of this section, I'm reminded of the old saying that the difference between a recession and depression is that an employed worker may feel he is in recession, however, an unemployed worker is certain he is in a depression.

Normand with his business degree in hand decided to change his career field and look for a job in the growing health care (hospital, etc.) administrative field. After months of rejection in his search, he applied for a job at the aerospace Loral Electronics Corporation in Yonkers, New York. The personnel manager there was a former KIC employee and a number of other employees who had been let go by KIC on Long Island were now employed by Loral.

I also made a half hearted attempt to change my career field. I applied for a few social services positions to no avail. I then searched for my drafting/designer field to no avail. I was now receiving unemployment benefits and Marta went back to work as a secretary to a partner in an accounting firm in Manhattan, NYC. It was at this time that I now occupied a new job category in the lexicon of job descriptions "Home Husband/Baby Sitter". Christopher was not quite a year old when I lost my job and Lesley had not yet started school. I, therefore, stayed home and became a "Home Dad". I watched the kids during the day and Marta took over in the evening hours. In January 1975 when I received my BA, I applied for and was accepted into C. W. Post College Graduate School with a major in History and Political Science. Four nights a week I would drive out to Long Island to attend classes while Marta held forth at home.

After a year of unemployment, I finally found a position as Chief Draftsman in a small motor manufacturing company called Ashland Electric Co. in L.I.C. I was in charge of a small drafting department of three draftsmen and my starting salary matched my salary when I left KIC.

1977 – 1979

In mid 1976, I applied to take an exam for employment with the Federal Government. It was called the PACE (Professional and Administrative Career Exam). I had waited until I received my degree because a college degree was required to take the exam. The day long test was in seven areas of expertise. A month or so later I received word of my grades and they were fairly high. In the meantime I was now employed by Ashland Electric. When almost a year passed and I received no further word from the federal government, I just forgot about the exam. One day in late October 1977, I received a telegram from the Defense Logistics Agency (DLA) in Manhattan to call for a job interview. I made an appointment the following day and went for an interview within the week. The position title was "Industrial Specialist" (IS) for the DLA which is an agency of the Department of Defense. When the interviewer saw my resume and discussed the requirements of the job, he stated that I had the background that he was looking for and explained the job requirements and salary, etc. He offered me the job and gave me a day to think it over and get back to him. Marta and I discussed it that night. The next day I accepted the job and gave Ashland a two week notice of my departure.

By 1977 our daughter Lesley was in second grade at the local grammar school and we had registered Christopher to attend "Little Friends" nursery school in Sunnyside, Queens. Every day a bus from Little Friends would pick him up and then drop him off at the end of the day. Christopher was to remain in that school through first grade and then we transferred him to Lesley's school, PS 76 in L. I.C.

Also in 1976 Marta registered for evening and weekend college at Elizabeth Seton College. Though the main campus was in Yonkers, NY, Marta attended a branch of the school in Manhattan. In May of 1978 Marta graduated with the degree of Associate in Arts. I was very proud of her. She had held down a responsible full time job, gone to school and managed our home with two young children.

Bob

By 1979 I had enough credits for my Master's Degree and only required to complete my Master's Thesis. I took a month's vacation from work, completed the research and writing of the thesis, submitted and defended the thesis to three professors and finally received the Masters of Arts degree in January 1980. I continued in my job at DLA as an IS and periodically was sent to government military schools at various military installations from Ohio to Virginia. Most of my courses were at the Air Force Institute of Technology at Wright Patterson Air Force Base in Dayton, Ohio. Some of the courses taken were as follows: Production Surveillance and Planning (7 weeks), Government Contract Administration (4 weeks), Contract Law (1 week), Quality Assurance (1 week), Government Packaging (1 week), Cost and Price Analysis (2 weeks), Contract Negotiations (1 week) and this list goes on. I was to work at DLA for 21 years and I once sat down and calculated that nearly two years of this time was spent in school. This fact and my prolonged college career prompted me to often say that I have been in school my entire life.

In 1983 I had taken enough courses to receive my Professional Designation in Contract Management issued jointly by the U.S. Air Force Air University and the National Contract Management Association (NCMA). I then applied for and received a new position as a Contract Administrator (CA) Where my IS position involved some contract work, the new CA position involved only contract administration work. The military contracts (Army, Navy, AF) were in the NYC, Long Island, Connecticut and Northern New Jersey areas. The IS job had been primarily a technical job where the CA job was primarily a contractual one.

In 1985 I applied for and received a "Staff" Contract Administrator position in the headquarters section of my agency (still located in our office in Manhattan). I remained in this position until 1987 when I applied for and was appointed to the position of Termination Contracting Officer (TCO). A TCO administers only contracts terminated for the convenience of the government. It is a warranted by the government position in that it gives the TCO the authority to sign for and spend the government's money for the settlement of terminated contracts. The change of position to TCO was just in time to witness the end of the U.S. and Russian military competition that was brought about by the political breakup of the USSR in 1989. The U.S. military began to terminate many of its military contracts all over the nation to realize savings on hardware no longer needed due to the decreased Russian threat. The need for additional TCOs (there had been only six TCOs for the entire New York, New Jersey, Connecticut area) became urgent and another five TCOs were added to the Termination Group. I was given responsibility for the new group of TCOs and remained in this position until I retired in October 1998.

Marta

In 1976 Marta's boss had taken a job as a partner in the large accounting firm of Coopers and Lybrand (C&L), also in Manhattan. Being very happy with Marta's expertise as his secretary, he asked her to come along with him to C&L with a raise in salary. His name was Barry Blazer and he was a young up and coming Actuary and was put in charge of the Actuary Department of C&L. Within a couple of years Barry was promoted to the position of Managing Partner which was a very significant position for a man still in his thirties.

In the middle 1980s Marta began taking a Computer Analyst course at New York University (NYU) in downtown Manhattan and by 1987 she had moved on to the Computer Department of C&L. She remained in this position until 1992.

Kathy

In the years after Barbara and I divorced, Kathy shuttled by airplane back and forth between Martinsville, Virginia and New York City as per our custody agreement. She would spend her entire summer vacations and Christmas vacations in New York and the rest of the year in Virginia attending grammar school and then Martinsville High School. The arrangement worked fairly well and Kathy seemed to enjoy her vacations in New York with her sister Lesley and brother Christopher. Kathy's mother had remarried but did not have any more children so Kathy was an only child in Virginia but a member of a larger family with Marta and myself. Each summer we would go on vacations to various places in the country and Kathy as well as the rest of the family enjoyed the travel. On at least three occasions we visited Marta's brother in Colorado. Three summer vacations were spent at a rental beach cottage on the "Jersey Shore", one summer we spent a week at a cottage on the Maine coast, three times we spent a week at a farm in Bucks County Pennsylvania and the list goes on.

In 1979 Kathy graduated from Martinsville High School. By this time her mother Barbara and husband Jim Bradsher had moved to the Washington D.C. area and Kathy moved with them. She obtained a job at the local People's Drug Store as a cashier. After a few months, she was to experience a dangerous situation which thankfully ended safely and positively. The store experienced an armed robbery for drugs. Recognizing the danger of the situation, the young pharmacist/manager advised Kathy to continue dealing with customers while he went to the back of the pharmacy to get the drugs for the thieves. The pharmacist's name was John Milom and after their mutual trial, Kathy and John started to go out on dates.

By early spring 1980 Kathy visited New York with John Milom to introduce him to Marta and myself. They planned to marry and were making plans for a wedding in early summer. Kathy made the plans and the wedding took place in Burke, Virginia at the Presbyterian Church. One of the ministers (there were two) performing the ceremony was John's brother-in-law. Lesley was a flower girl in the wedding party and Christopher was the ring bearer. One of the maids of honor was Kathy's good friend from Long Island City, Doris Milan. We all had a good time at the reception.

Kathy and John rented a town house in Burke, Virginia and then purchased another town house in Springfield, Virginia. Over a period of eight years they were to have four daughters: Melissa, born January 30, 1981 (on Kathy's own birthday), Jacqueline, born September 24, 1982, Jessica, born November 17, 1986 and Amanda, born November 10, 1988. Due to the increasing need for more space, Kathy and John were to purchase and move into two more houses in the 1980's, both in Manassas, Virginia. Both of these houses were larger unattached homes on two acres of property in a then rural area of Manassas.

Lesley and Christopher

Lesley was to graduate from grammar school (PS 176) in 1978 and Christopher four years later in 1980. Lesley was to go to a Junior High School in Astoria for two more years and then transfer to LaGuardia High School located a few blocks from our home in L.I.C. Christopher was to spend his first two years of high school at Saint Demetrious Greek Orthodox School in Astoria, Queens. Marta and I felt that he should be exposed to some of his mother's Greek culture in his formative years. At St. Demetrious (St. Ds) he was to take Greek language as well as Greek history and culture courses as well as all the other usual high school courses. While he was in St. Ds, he joined the church sponsored Boy Scout troop and this was a positive influence during his early teen years (14 through 16).

As was true for many American families, the teen years for

our family in the 1980s were very difficult, both for Lesley and Christopher and ultimately for Marta and myself. After doing very well in St. Ds, Christopher prevailed on us to transfer him to the local public high school, Long Island City High School (LICHS). He did moderately well at LICHS for the first semester but then began to act out and cut classes. Before this period, Lesley had begun to cut her classes and had lost complete interest in school. It was as if Christopher had seen Lesley's bad behavior and decided to imitate this behavior. Between 1986 and 1990 Marta and I found ourselves completely overwhelmed by our kids. I won't go into the painful details of our battle but suffice it to say that I'm happy to announce we apparently all survived the experience. However, we all have the scars from our trials and our children, particularly Lesley, are still dealing with the consequences.

1988 - 1992

The last two years of the 1980s and the first two years of the 90s were to bring great changes to our family. After three years of struggle in high school, Lesley turned eighteen in 1988 and now dropped out of school. Shortly thereafter, she left home and moved up to central New York (New Berlin) to live with her boyfriend.

On May 31, 1990, Marta's mother Mary died at her home in Albuquerque, New Mexico. The entire family gathered in N.M. to attend her funeral. On April 31, 1991, almost exactly a year to the day after Mary's death, Christopher was operated on for testicular cancer. He was just seventeen years old. A few weeks of radiation treatment followed. When Christopher returned to high school he had lost complete interest in school and he dropped out.

In October, 1991, Marta and I bought and closed on a vacation/retirement Victorian farmhouse in New Berlin, New York. We had for a few years been searching for a home in "the country" with the aim of using it as a future retirement home. A visit to Lesley in New Berlin in the summer of 1990 had acquainted us with the beauty of upstate New York. Between October 1991 and the summer of 1992, Marta and I would spend each weekend working on our farmhouse. We hired a contractor to perform major renovations (outside painting, new plumbing, updated electric, etc.) and proceeded to decorate and paint the interior ourselves.

By the summer of 1991, Christopher had recovered from his illness and recognized the need for continuing his education. He took a high school GED exam and passed. He then applied for and was accepted by the Borough of Manhattan Community College. His major was Communications and Video. In June of 1995 he graduated with the Degree of Associate of Applied Science. His overall grade Point Average (GPA) had been over 3.5; quite a change from his high school difficulties. Marta and I believe his life threatening cancer had resolved him to do something with his life. Christopher then registered for Brooklyn College (CUNY) with a major in Film Production and ultimately graduated with a Bachelor of Arts degree.

In the fall of 1992, we were surprisingly presented with bad news. Though there had been no advanced indication by Coopers and Lybrand, Marta was notified that she was being let go. She had been with the company for seventeen years and had progressed from Secretary of a Managing Partner to a Senior Computer Analyst. She was at that time the only one let go in her group. A co-worker in her group advised her that a few months later her position was replaced with a recent college graduate (a man), surely for a much lower salary. By the time of her layoff Marta had progressed to a respectable salary. Marta's friend and co-worker advised her to file an age and sex discrimination case against "Coopers", however, she decided to forego that option.

Now that Marta was not working, she decided to live in our newly renovated house in New Berlin. Since I wished to work for a few more years before retirement, I continued to live in our L.I.C. apartment and would commute on weekends upstate and return to N.Y.C. on Monday evenings (by this time in my career I chose to take three day weekends).

1993 – 1998

Between 1993 and 1998 I continued to commute on weekends between New York City and New Berlin in upstate New York. Marta found temporary work doing taxes for H & R Block in New Berlin and then found permanent employment for Circulars Unlimited in Norwich, N.Y. as a typesetter. By this time, the technology of typesetting had progressed from a physical typewriter generating type letters to a computer word processing screen environment. Marta worked at Circulars Unlimited until 1995 when she obtained a civil service position with the Department of Social Services. After a couple of years Marta Became the secretary to the Commissioner of Social Services.

Lesley by 1995 had moved with her boyfriend to Cape May, New Jersey. She subsequently broke up with this boyfriend but continued to live and work in Cape May. She worked in a hotel doing housekeeping in the warm weather months and finally obtained a year around position in a Victorian Bed and Breakfast. By 1997 she had a new boyfriend named John McQuillan, an accomplished carpenter who was working on restoration projects in the many Victorian buildings located in Cape May.

After a number of positions in the video/communications/audio visual services industry, in 2000 Christopher settled into a position at the Hudson Hotel in New York City, working for a company called PSAV (Presentation Services Audio Visual). Rather than endure the low pay entry level intern positions in the NYC film industry, Christopher opted for a nine to five, well paying, fairly secure audio visual position.

As for myself, by 1994 my TCO position at DLA had been

moved from a federal building in Greenwich Village, NYC to Fort Wadsworth in Staten Island. A 25 minute subway ride from L.I.C. to "the Village" had become a costly and time consuming (approximately 1 ½ hours) trip to Staten Island. I decided it would be wise to endure the inconvenience of another four years until I reached the age of 65. I would then be able to retire from the government with Medicare medical coverage.

An Air Force Reunion

Early in September 1996 Marta and I flew to Colorado Springs, Colorado to attend a reunion of the 8th FBW Korean veterans. On September 5, we attended a Memorial Plaque Dedication at the Air Force Academy Military Cemetery. For the next four days we enjoyed ourselves sightseeing in the area and attending various reunion events. One very exciting event was our drive up the winding dirt road that climbs to the top of Pike's Peak at over 14,000 feet. Marta enjoyed our day spent in Cripple Creek, Colorado which is an old mining town now completely dedicated to gambling casinos. After the four days of reunion events, we attended a reunion banquet on the last night. The dance music was supplied by members of the Air Force band. Marta and I then drove up to Fort Collins, Colorado to visit Marta's brother Tony and his family. We jointly rented a cabin for a week in the Rocky Mountains and enjoyed fishing and sightseeing in the area. Returning our rented car to Colorado Springs, we reluctantly flew back to New York.

CHAPTER **17**

Life After Retirement 1998 – 2006

In April 1998 Marta and I drove to New York City and then flew to Aruba in the Caribbean with our best friends Richie and Dottie Cesaro from Long Island, NY. We stayed in a beautiful beachside hotel which included Marta's mandatory gambling casino. We celebrated our 30th wedding anniversary on April 28th while in Aruba. Dottie and Richie's 30th wedding anniversary occurred on June 15, a little over a month later. Marta and Dottie had been best friends for over 30 years, dating back to when they both worked for Kollsman Instrument Corp.

I retired from the Department of Defense on October 3, 1998. My first weekend of retirement was spent with Marta, Dottie and Richie at a four day Oktoberfest weekend at Canoe Island Lodge in Lake George, N.Y. For the last ten years we and the Cesaros had been attending Oktoberfest weekends at least every other year at Lake George. The owner of the Canoe Island Lodge, Bill Bush, graciously presented me with a retirement cake for the occasion. My first week of retirement was "wonderful".

A Family Reunion

Within a few days upon returning from Lake George, Marta and I attended a Tellier family reunion in Woonsocket, Rhode Island.

My cousin Gene Peloquin (Mom's sister Louise Tellier's son) had dedicated a podium to the Woonsocket Museum of Work and Culture in his father's honor (Armond Peloquin). Gene took the occasion to invite all of the Tellier family to the catered occasion. The last time the Tellier family had gotten together was at a 90th birthday party the cousins had thrown for Uncle Ernest Villeneuve in Oxbridge, Mass. on June 23, 1991. Sadly, this Tellier get-together in October 1998 was the last time we were to see Uncle Ernest. He died in December 1998, just six months short of his 98th birthday. Mom was now the last of her generation still alive. She was 95 years old at this time.

While on this visit to Rhode Island, I took the opportunity to visit some of the Woonsocket sites of my Mom's youth. The "Alice Mill" where Mom worked in 1917 is still standing and is now recycled as an electronics manufacturing company. The armory where Mom met Dad is also still standing and looks much as it did in my parent's day. The apartment house where Mom lived with her sister (Aunt Marion) and its surroundings look much the same. I am indebted to my cousin Cecile Dubeau (Marion's daughter) for my nostalgic Rhode Island tour.

Lesley Moves to the LIC House

For the next few weeks upon returning from Rhode Island, Marta and I helped move our daughter Lesley and her boyfriend John from their apartment in Seaside Heights, New Jersey to our second floor apartment in Mom's Long Island City house. Our son Christopher was to subsequently move from this second floor apartment to Mom's third floor apartment when Mom decided to move in permanently with my sister Connie on the first floor. At 95 years old, climbing two flights of stairs to the third floor had become beyond Mom's ability. Additionally, by this time Connie was cooking all their meals and was in effect taking care of Mom in all matters.

Genesis of "The Book"

Shortly after the Christmas holidays in early 1999, I began the project which had been evolving in my mind since the early 1970s. That project was the research and telling of the story of both my families, the Telliers and the Brunelles. Actually the enterprise had entered my mind as early as 1962 – 1965 when I was living in Boston. Many weekends I would visit Uncle Ernest in Woonsocket, R.I. which was just a short distance (40 miles) from my apartment in West Boston. Uncle Ernest and I talked in great length about the family and, being an elder of the family at that time, he was very knowledgeable. I asked him about his and my mom's generation and about the generation that came before them. Shortly upon returning to live in LIC in 1966, I received a large brown envelope from Uncle Ernest and in it I found a listing of all the members of his generation and the generation before his (my grandfather Tellier's brothers and sisters). Though the responsibilities of a career and raising a family took precedence over my intended project, I told myself I would begin the family book as soon as I retired. Consequently, in early 1999 I began research for the book. By 2000, though the research was far from complete, I began writing the Tellier – Brunelle story.

A nephew marries

In September of 2000 we returned again to Colorado for a couple of weeks. Marta's nephew Kenny Babb (her brother Tony's son) was getting married to a girl named Chelsea. Her parents had a small ranch in the mountains and rather than arrive before the preacher in a limousine, they arrived in a two horse pulled buckboard. The reception was held at the ranch and we all had an old fashioned good time. Daughter Lesley and boyfriend John came with us but son Christopher was unable to get time off.

A Death in the Family

On the 18th of April 2001, brother Normand called me to say that his wife Nancy had died. She had been in the hospital in Glen Cove, Long Island for a couple of weeks and had returned home the day before she died. Nancy had been a semi invalid for many years having had a stroke in her forties from which she never fully recovered. Marta and I drove downstate to attend the funeral services which took place in Glen Cove. Burial took place in Roslyn Cemetery on Long Island.

Las Vegas

Now that I was retired and living together full time with Marta in New Berlin, New York, we decided to start going places and doing things we wanted to do for years but never had the opportunity. Though we had visited the gambling casinos in Atlantic City many times, Marta had always wanted to visit Las Vegas, Nevada. In May of 2001 we finally decided to make the trip and flew from Albany, NY to Vegas. Renting a car, we were able to gamble at an average of two casinos per day. At the end of the week, I counted sixteen casinos that we had visited. Though we did not make any money, Marta was in "seventh heaven".

A Return to the Tellier Roots

By the fall of 2001, my efforts in the family research had generated a curiosity in me about the town in Canada where Mom was born in 1903. By this time I had almost completed the research for the first Tellier in Canada and his descendants. I pretty much knew where they had lived and died, including Mom's place of birth, St. Cuthbert, Province of Quebec. On September 7, 2001, we began our trip to Canada.

When we had almost reached the St. Lawrence river, we headed east and drove to the small town of St. Ours ("ooze") (see Chapter 3) on the Richelieu River. This is the place that Jean Baptiste LeTellier had his first farm upon leaving the French army in 1668. It was a strange but wonderful feeling to be walking the land where my maternal ancestor had settled exactly three hundred and thirty three (333) years earlier

From St. Ours, we drove a few miles to the town of Varennes (Chapter 3) which like St. Ours is on the south side of the St. Lawrence River. It was here that Jean Baptiste LeTellier died in 1704. I looked through the local cemetery but was unable to find any ancestors. We next headed to the St. Lawrence River and at the town of Sorel we put the car on a ferry and took a short river crossing to the town of Berthier. Staying for the night in a local motel, we drove the next day to St. Cuthbert. The reader may recall this small town of my Mom's birth from the description I give in Chapter 7.

The next couple of days were spent visiting Montreal and St. Joseph's Oratory on Mount Royal overlooking the city. Again, the reader may recall my description of the founder of St. Joseph's, Brother Andre' (Uncle Ernest's Great Uncle – see Chapter 9). Marta and I stood in Brother Andre's austere bedroom which has been preserved in the modest 1917 era chapel that preceded the present church. Again I felt I was standing in the footsteps of family history.

While in Montreal (on September 10, 2001) we visited the casino on an island adjacent to the old Montreal shore. The building housing the casino had been a hold-over building from the 1967 World's Fair. Marta enjoyed a few hours of gambling and we then proceeded to drive home to New York. We crossed the Canada/US border into New York around 7:00 P.M. on September 10, 2001 and arrived home around midnight. The next day Marta returned to work at the Chenango County Department of Social Services and I brought our car (a newly purchased 2001 Chrysler PT Cruiser) in for an early morning service call.

September 11 (9/11)

On September 11, 2001 Christopher went up on the roof of our LIC home (a three story building) to witness what was happening at the World Trade Center two miles away as the crow flies. Christopher called on his cell phone to tell me to turn on the TV, however, I was at the Chrysler dealer so he proceeded to leave me a message. As he was describing what he was witnessing, the north tower of the World Trade Center collapsed. The message Christopher left on my answering machine reminds me of the famous eye witness radio description of the Hindenburg disaster. Since our LIC home is directly across the street from the 50 story Citicorp Building, the entire family (Christopher, Lesley, John, Mom and my sister Connie) became very concerned that our neighboring skyscraper was now a target. The NYC police and Citicorp management proceeded to increase security surveillance on the building. Marta and I drove down to NYC the following weekend to give the kids some comfort and assurance.

A Trip to Marta's Roots

In early 2002, Marta and I finally decided to make the trip to Greece that we had long planned but never made. Our good friends Jay and Litsa Moore from LIC had been making the trip at least every other year since their marriage in 1970. Litsa was born in Greece and had family there. Each year they would invite us to accompany them. In 2002 we surprised them by saying "Yes". As I mentioned in the introduction to the book, Marta's maternal ancestry dates back to Greece. Her Mother's parents had settled in NYC in the early part of the 1900s. Litsa and Marta meticulously planned our trip and itinerary, making airline, hotel reservations, etc. Over the years, Marta had received very little information about her grandparents besides the fact that her grandfather, James Christopoulos, was a Greek who came from Constantinople and her Grandmother Anna Nikitas had come from a small Greek island called Siros in the Aegean Sea.

Upon arriving in Greece, we spent a few days sightseeing in Athens and then took a ferry (ship) from the port of Peiraias to Siros, a voyage of about seven hours. As the ship approached the harbor of Hermoupolis, the main town of Siros, we were excited by the beauty of the scene before us. Overlooking the main town are two large hills dominated by ancient church steeples. The left hill contains the medieval town of Ano Syros which was established in the 8th century. We were to learn later that this hilltop settlement offered its inhabitants protection from all kinds of invaders including pirates. The island has been invaded by Phoenicians, Cretans, Ionians, Athenians, Romans, Byzantines, Venetians, Franks and Turks. Excavations on the island found traces of human life from the Bronze Age over 3000 years ago. In the 19th century, Syros became a wealthy and powerful port in the eastern Mediterranean.

Marta and Litsa had made reservations in a beautiful mansion turned hotel that overlooked the harbor and the sea. We were to spend four days in Siros sightseeing all the historical and wonderful sights but the highlight of our tour occurred on the second day when we visited the town hall in Hermoupolis, the largest town on Siros.

The town hall built in the 19th century is a beautiful stone building that is more imposing and larger than City Hall in NYC. Since marble is so readily available in Greece, much of the interior is handsome marble columns and floors. (Even the streets in Hermoupolis are paved with marble.) We searched out the room that contained the records of the island and were directed to an area on the left end of the building. Upon entering the first room we were confronted by stacks of record volumes from floor to high ceiling. Since our object was to research Marta's grandmother, we immediately thought we had an impossible searching task before us. Upon entering the next room, we were to find two ladies, one of whom was sitting in front of a computer. We explained the reason for our visit and Marta gave the lady her grandmother's name. Within an instant, the lady had located Anna Nikitas' birth certificate information on the computer. The certificate contained much information such as parents names, dates, place of birth, siblings, etc. Giving us a printout, she then proceeded to go into the next room with the original record volumes, locate the proper volume and then made us a copy of the original. The only other time I have seen Marta as happy is when she won $1,000 on a slot machine. (Thank God for the computer age!!)

Telling this story reminds me that Marta did find a small gambling casino on Siros and she joyfully gambled on the very Greek island where her grandmother Anna Nikitos was born in 1894.

We returned to Peiraias/Athens by the way we had come, the ship ferry. We then spent a few more days exploring Athens, again visiting the Acropolis and a couple of museums. One of the most interesting places we visited was the ancient Athens marketplace called the Agora. It was here that the Greek philosophers such as Plato and Aristotle had their famous discourses.

We next rented a car for a week and proceeded to drive around the Peloponnese. Our destination was the town of Kyparissia where Litsa had lived as a child and where she had inherited (and still owned) her parents home. Spending a few days in Litsa's home, we made daily trips to other famous sites in Greece such as Olympia where the Olympic games were first held in the 7th century B.C.

Upon leaving Kyparissia, we continued around the Peloponnese, staying a night and one day in the medieval fortress town called Monemvasia located on the Aegean Sea. We then drove back to Athens and reluctantly flew back to the U.S.

2002 - 2003

The summer of 2002 was spent gardening around the house and enjoying our country life. Marta still had two weeks vacation coming from her job at Chenango County Social Services so we decided to visit her Greek cousin Kathy in Virginia Beach, Virginia. Marta is godmother to Kathy and Billy Santos' daughter Anastasia. After spending a few days with Kathy, we then drove to Manassas, Virginia to visit my daughter Kathy and grandchildren. Starting with the spring visit to Greece and ending with our visit to Kathy had made for a perfect summer.

In mid September, we again went to an Oktoberfest weekend at Lake George, New York. Richie and Dottie Cesaro also joined us as did Richie's cousin Eddie and his wife Carol. Marta and I were taken aback by Dottie's appearance when we saw her. For the last six years Dottie had been fighting breast cancer and though it had been in remission for the last couple of years, it had returned again. Though Marta and Dottie had continued their friendship by weekly telephone conversations, Marta was not aware of how bad the medical situation had become. For her part, Dottie did not want to back out of our previously planned Oktoberfest weekend. When Dottie was unable to attend our Saturday night dinner and dance, Richie tearfully told us that the doctors had said that they could no longer help Dottie and that the end was near. We all parted Sunday afternoon after dinner to return home; Richie, Dottie, Eddie and Carol to their Long Island, New York homes and Marta and I to our home in central New York. It was a sad parting since we did not expect we would see Dottie again. Dottie died October 5, 2002, just a few weeks after our Oktoberfest weekend.

Before we left for the Oktoberfest weekend, Marta had complained about stomach problems and the doctor had sent her for tests and CAT scans. Upon returning home, Marta went to see the doctor to obtain the results of the tests. The diagnosis was devastating. Marta had cancer of the Pancreas. Marta promptly researched pancreatic cancer on the computer to supplement the information she received from our General Practitioner. When we visited a surgeon at Basset Hospital to see if the cancer was operable, Marta had a pretty clear idea of the seriousness of the cancer. Not having seen Marta's computer information, I was pretty much uninformed. Upon reviewing the tests and CT scans, the surgeon concluded that the cancer was inoperable. He advised us that we could get a second opinion but gave no further recommendation. Marta asked him how long she had to live and the surgeon gave an obviously evasive answer. We did receive a second opinion from the oncology people at John Hopkins Hospital in Maryland and the conclusion was the same.

Marta requested to see a local oncologist and opted to undergo chemotherapy and radiation treatments. No recommendation was given by the oncologist which led us to suspect the doctors had concluded she didn't have long to live. The oncologist also made clear to us that the treatments would not eliminate the cancer and that ultimately the illness was terminal.

Over the next thirteen months, Marta put up a brave and valiant fight. She continued to work for a few months while receiving portable chemotherapy treatments (24/7). We spent a couple of weeks in Florida in April 2003, staying at Richie Cesaro's condo in Sarasota. Her condition continued to decline over the summer and she spent the entire month of September in Bassett Hospital in Cooperstown. She returned home on the 30th of September and received Hospice assistance.

Marta died at 8:25 A.M. on the 17th of October 2003. Our daughter Lesley and son Christopher were present at the end. The funeral service was conducted at the Greek Orthodox Church of the Resurrection in Glen Cove, Long Island and burial was at Roslyn Cemetery nearby. A few weeks later, we had a memorial service for her at the United Methodist Church in New Berlin, allowing some of her co-workers and friends to remember her. Marta was 59 years old when she died.

2004 - 2006

Coming only 2 ½ months after Marta's death, the Christmas of 2003 was very difficult for myself, Christopher and Lesley. Christopher and I drove to Kathy's house in Virginia for the holidays and had the comfort of being with family.

In the early summer of 2004, the family was again visited by tragedy. Marta's stepsister Valerie lost her 21 year old daughter Laura to a military service murder. As a sailor stationed on the aircraft carrier Theodore Roosevelt, she was living in port in Virginia while the ship was being refitted. One of her shipmates from her department killed her for no apparent reason and then attempted to dispose of her body. The funeral was to take place in Florida and Chris, Lesley and I made airline reservations to go. Four days before our flight to Florida, Normand's daughter Christiane lost her daughter Grace Ann. Though Grace Ann had been born with serious medical problems, her mother had gone through extraordinary measures to care for her during her three short years of life. Grace Ann was buried in Roslyn Cemetery on Long Island on June 3, 2004. The next day we flew to Orlando, Florida for Laura Skinner's funeral. Laura was buried on June 6, 2004.

Mom's 101st birthday was on June 4, 2004. We had planned to celebrate on that day but Grace Ann's and Laura's deaths had delayed our plans. Upon returning to Long Island City after Laura's funeral, we had a small family gathering on June 8th to celebrate Mom's birthday. Coincidently, June 8th is my birthday so the family got a birthday cake with both our names on it. I have always gauged my age by Mom's age since she was exactly 30 years and four days old when I was born. Therefore, I quickly determined my own age as 71 (101 minus 30). The more elderly readers of this passage may identify with my age determination dilemma. As I have gotten older, I honestly can't remember exactly how old I am. (I usually calculate a year less.)

We had always said to Mom to hang in there and she would

break the 100 year old barrier. All agreed that achieving 101 years was a major achievement of Mom's. Unfortunately it became apparent to all attending the birthday that Mom's health was declining. She no longer had her vision and her hearing was very bad. Fortunately her mind was still very keen and her incredible memory was still intact. Each time I visited her from upstate, she would ask me to read from the family story. By 2004, I was up to approximately 1945 in the Brunelle/Tellier saga.

In July 2004, Christopher and I embarked on one last cross country road trip west. We had decided to drive to Albuquerque, New Mexico to visit Marta's stepfather, Ken Wassmer. He was now living alone since Marta's mother's death in 1990. It was by way of a last sentimental journey by car. We had driven to Colorado in 1977 and 1978 to visit Marta's brother Tony and his family, but after those years we had always flown. When we visited Marta's parents in New Mexico, we had flown there. On one occasion only, we flew to Tony's home in Colorado and rented a car and drove the 500 miles south to Albuquerque.

Chris and I greatly enjoyed this 2004 trip. We pretended we were the two guys (actors Martin Milner and George Maharis) driving casually on the old Route 66 and having adventures along the way. We even simulated the car from their TV series "Route 66". Of course, we did not have their convertible Chevy Corvette but we did roll back the sun roof on our 2001 PT Cruiser. On many occasions, Christopher would hold up his video camera and film from the opening in the roof. We stopped off one morning in Dayton, Ohio to see the great Air Force Museum at Wright Patterson AFB. I had visited there often when my job with the government had sent me to school at "Wright Patterson". Going southwest and then west on Interstate 44, we were paralleling the old Route 66 and occasionally would get off I44 and drive a few miles on the old road. Great fun!!

The trip's real benefit, however, was the bond Chris and I formed on this journey. The family deaths of the past year had left us totally drained and depressed and our youthful abandon on this trip was needed and appreciated.

We enjoyed a week's stay with Ken in New Mexico, revisiting many historical sights we had visited with Marta. The visit was "bittersweet". It is fortunate we made this visit because in 2005, Ken sold his house and moved to Orlando, Florida to be near his daughter Valerie and son Ronnie. Chris and I then drove north to visit Marta's brother "Uncle Tony", stayed a few days and then drove back east to New York. It had been a wonderful vacation for us both.

In the fall of 2004 I began taking a grief counseling workshop sponsored by the Chenango County Hospice. Though it had been almost a year since Marta's death, I felt I required some help in dealing with issues of death and mortality. I had attended monthly grief support meetings at Hospice during the summer and upon completion of the six sessions course (one night a week), I began to attend a Wednesday night social dinner with members of the Hospice group. We had all interacted so well in the counseling group that we wanted to keep in contact in a social setting. By Christmas 2004, Shirley Niles (a member of the workshop previous to my own and also a member of the Wednesday night group) and I began seeing each other socially outside the group. Aside from the fact that we had both lost spouses to cancer, we found that we had many other things in common. I will advise the reader of one significant commonality we have. Like myself, Shirley and I are both interested in genealogy and family history. When I showed her my family genealogy chart and my uncompleted family history (the book) she told me she also planned to write her family story. We began to help each other by using each other's expertise. I generated genealogy charts for Shirley's family and she expertly typed and edited my family manuscript. The book you are now reading would never have materialized without Shirley's generous assistance. I hereby belatedly add Shirley Niles name to all my family and friends enumerated in the

ACKNOWLEDGEMENTS preceding Chapter One.

In late November, I received word from sister Connie that Mom's health was failing. She had refused to eat properly for weeks despite Connie's best efforts to feed her. The doctor had found her totally dehydrated and recommended she be hospitalized. She was to spend one week in Astoria General Hospital in Queens and died on December 3, 2004. Her great heart had survived and witnessed the better (and worst) part of the 20th century.

As per Mom's wishes, we did not have a funeral. Her body was cremated and a month later, we had a memorial service at her church with all of her friends present. Her ashes were subsequently buried with Dad's ashes at Roslyn Cemetery. Nancy (Mattson) Brunelle, Marta (Babb) Brunelle, Harvey Joseph Brunelle and Alice (Tellier) Brunelle rest next to each other in a quiet rural setting on Long Island, New York. Christiane (Brunelle) Murphy's young daughter Grace Ann lies a few yards away.

On February 17, 2006, the family suffered another tragic loss. Marta's brother Tony Babb (her only sibling) suffered a fatal heart attack. He was 59 years old, the same age as Marta was when she died. As per Tony's family's wishes, he was cremated at his hometown of Fort Collins, Colorado. His family (wife Barbara, son Kenny and daughter Stacy) decided to forego a formal funeral. A memorial service would be held in the summer at which time Christopher and I would attend.

On July 1, 2006, Christopher and I began our second auto trip west. This time we were heading directly to Colorado to attend Tony's memorial service. We arrived in Steamboat Springs, Colorado at Kenny's home on July 4th where the rest of the Babb family had assembled. We then proceeded to a campsite in the Rocky Mountains which had been Tony's favorite camping spot. We set up a comfortable camp and the next day proceeded to a mountain stream which was much loved by Tony. After saying prayers and recalling favorite stories of Tony's life, his wife Barbara and children Kenny and Stacy gently put Tony's ashes into the stream. We all cried as Tony's remains mingled and disappeared into the rapid waters.

    Christopher and I remained with the Babbs for a week and then proceeded to Montana to visit the site of Custer's Last Stand. We then drove east, visiting Devil's Tower in Wyoming, Mount Rushmore, Deadwood and The Badlands National Park in South Dakota. On the way through Red Cloud, Nebraska, we stopped off to visit Willa Cather's childhood home (see the reference to Willa Cather in ACKNOWLEDGEMENTS). After five days of eastward wandering, we arrived back home in New York

CHAPTER **18**

Harvey and Alice Brunelle's Grandchildren and Great Grandchildren - 2009

As previously mentioned, my brother Normand has four children: Anders, Guy, Kyle and Christiane. These children in turn have a total of eight children of their own. (Guy has three and Christiane has five.) I have three children: Kathy, Lesley and Christopher. Kathy (my only married child) has five children. Therefore, the total count of grandchildren for Alice and Harvey stands at seven. This is far less than the fifty-three grandchildren of Mom's parents Joseph Tellier and Angelina Durand Tellier. The total count of great grandchildren stands at thirteen and is definitely less than the hundred plus great grandchildren of Joseph and Angelina. Clearly, the American family size has decreased significantly in the last century. We have gone from the rural agricultural society of my grandparents day to the industrialized, highly technical urban and suburban society of the present day. No comment on this change is really necessary; it is just a fact of life. As of this writing (2009), the status of Normand Brunelle's children is as follows:

Anders Brunelle

Anders is now 53 years old. After high school he attended Hofstra University on Long Island and obtained a bachelor's degree in Engineering. He has been employed as an environmental engineer for many years and has pursued his hobby of accumulating, repairing and driving old cars (he presently has 18 cars). In addition to his car hobby, he is involved in real estate on Long Island and presently owns and rents out three private homes. Remaining single until 2008, he married Felix "Maruja" Cortez. She is a native of Peru. They have no children.

Guy Brunelle

Guy is now 51 years old. After high school, he worked for a few years in a Long Island nursing home. He then applied for and was accepted in the Police Academy in New York City. Upon graduation, he was assigned to the 115th Precinct in the Borough of Queens. He occupied this position for a decade, receiving many decorations and awards. In 1995, while responding to a call for help from a rape victim, he was shot by the perpetrator. After recovering, he received the NYC Police Department's bravery award from the then mayor David Denkins. He left the Police Department, retiring on a disability pension. He is married to Patricia Lagos and they have three children: Bianca (born October 19, 1993, Adrien (born July 7, 2003) and Collette (born April 26, 2005). They presently live on Long Island.

Kyle Brunelle

Kyle is presently 49 years old. After high school he attended college at Webb Institute in Glen Cove, Long Island where he received a degree in Naval Architecture. Upon graduation, he moved to California and worked in his profession at the U.S. Naval Shipyard in Vallejo, outside San Francisco. After a decade of working for the government, the shipyard was closed and Kyle studied for and obtained his professional engineer's license. He then obtained a position with the Port of Oakland. Like his brothers Anders and Guy, Kyle married in middle age. He is married to Deborah Raush. They have no children. Kyle and Deborah live in the San Francisco area.

Christiane Brunelle Murphy

Chris is now 44 and is married to Kevin Murphy. Until 2008 they lived in Glen Cove, Long Island. They have five children:
1. Kevin, born August 21, 1996
2. Katherine, born March 31, 1998
3. Luke, born August 1, 1999
4. Grace Ann, born May 20, 2001 and deceased May 30, 2004
5. Mary, born August 14, 2002
6. James, born August 27, 2004

Chris has been an excellent homemaker and mother for most of her adult life and has adopted motherhood as the highest calling. Upon the birth of her fourth child she struggled to care for this seriously ill girl and her other four children. Sadly, Grace Ann died shortly before Chris had her sixth child. Husband Kevin's job necessitated that they move to Georgia in 2008 and subsequently they have relocated to Orlando, Florida.

The status of my (Bob Brunelle's) children is as follows:

Kathy Brunelle Milom Hellin

Kathy is now 48 years old. After high school graduation she worked in a drug store where she met her husband John Milom. She and John lived in Virginia and had four daughters:
1. Melissa, born January 30, 1981
2. Jacqueline, born September 24, 1982

3. Jessica, born November 17, 1986
4. Amanda, born November 10, 1988.

After 20 years of marriage and having raised four daughters, Kathy and her husband John Milom divorced. She then married Keith Hellin. They have a son named Cody born on May 2, 2002. Kathy had worked in a real estate office and later became a licensed real estate agent.

Cody began first grade in September 2008. Kathy's daughters Melissa, Jessica and Amanda are all as yet single and attend college in Richmond, Virginia. Her daughter Jacqueline (also single) has a day job but is also a writer and poet. She published her first book of poems in 2008 called "Writing Letters to Morrison".

Lesley Brunelle

Lesley is now 38 years old. After high school, she lived in New Berlin, New York with her first boyfriend. They later moved to New Jersey. She subsequently broke up with him and was working at a beautiful victorian bed and breakfast in Cape May when she met her current boyfriend John McQuillan, a talented carpenter. They moved to New York City and she continues to live in the Brunelle Long Island City House in Queens with her boyfriend John. They have been together over twelve years and like many of today's younger generation have chosen not to marry. Lesley has recently reflected on her youthful withdrawal from high school and returned to community college. She is still uncertain what career path she would like to pursue.

Christopher Brunelle

Chris is presently 35 years old. After high school, Christopher received his Associates' Degree in Applied Science – Communications and Video from the Borough of Manhattan Community College (CUNY). He then went on to Brooklyn College

(CUNY) to receive a bachelor of arts degree with a major in film production. He worked as a Senior Event Technology Specialist for Event Presentation Services Company at the Hudson Hotel in New York for several years. He became engaged to be married to a German girl named Birgitta Petersson in 2007. Chris moved to Germany in October, 2007. He worked in Munich until May of 2009. He is presently living and working in Berlin. Birgitta is a graduate of Berlin Fashion College and is currently attending graduate school in Berlin majoring in business and economics. The Event Presentation Services company that Chris works for is the German affiliate of the same company he worked for in New York City. After marriage, they plan to continue living in Germany.

Epilogue

The Tellier and Brunelle story has been a long journey, both in the living and the telling. The living story began in 1665 with two French soldiers transported to New France in the Americas. The writing and telling of their story began at the start of the new millennium in the year 2002 and is concluding now in the year 2009.

The family and the world have experienced and survived many changes since 1665 and I am sure that the two French soldiers would be complete aliens in the modern world. Although this is true, it must be noted that the French speaking peoples in the United States continued to cling to their language, religion and culture right up to World War II.

The continuance of the French culture in the U.S. is no longer the case. While most of my 52 first cousins on my mother's side married French speaking spouses, their children and mine have married many other nationalities and religions. I and my surviving cousins (18 at last count) are the last generation of totally French Canadian Americans. The language and the Catholic Church of our youth that was the glue that held the culture together in Woonsocket, Rhode Island and the New England communities is now almost gone. The French speaking parochial schools no longer exist and the French speaking masses are in the past. The Cathedral of St. Ann's that my mother and the rest of her family attended is now converted to a museum. The Franco American culture that I describe in the introduction will be gone when my generation has passed.

If there is one element of life that runs throughout my family story and throughout history in general, it is CHANGE. My ancestors and the rest of humanity have witnessed and lived through incredible changes. We have survived illness, epidemics, personal tragedies, wars, economic calamities, dislocation and every adversity imaginable. Just as exposure to and survival of an illness can bring subsequent immunity to that illness, I believe the family will continue to survive and prosper despite adverse changes.

Just three years ago, I wrote Chapter Nine describing my parents difficulties during the "Great Depression" of 1929 – 1940. As I write this epilogue, the U.S. and the world are in the midst of the greatest financial crisis since the start of the 1929 depression. Our government advises us that if it had not spent billions of dollars rescuing banks and other institutions, our capitalist system as we know it would have suffered a complete failure. Furthermore, the seventy four year old venerable Chrysler Corporation that produced my grandfather's 1925 Chrysler touring car and my father's 1929 Chrysler sedan has gone into bankruptcy and is forced to merge with Fiat Motors to survive.

In the political arena, the Korean War which I describe in Chapter Thirteen is still unsettled fifty six years after a truce was signed in 1953. The present North Korean leader Kim Jong Il (who is the son of Kim Il Sung, the leader during the Korean war) continues to act aggressively by testing nuclear bombs and long range missiles.

In all of the above, it seems that the more things have changed over the years, the more they have remained the same. Have we not learned any lessons from history? I am reminded of a very wise statement my mother made in a 1992 video my son

Christopher made of Grandma. When Christopher asked her what she thought of life today, she answered "I'm for progress and change but only if the change is for the better." Mother had much wisdom and the more I observe life and world events, I wonder as she did if we are changing for the better.

In conclusion, I bequeath our family story to my descendants with the hope that some enjoyment and benefit may be gained from its telling. As historian and author Adam Gopnik has said "We are all pebbles dropped in the sea of history." [4*]

JRB
6/14/09

---

4 *"Twin Peaks ", Smithsonian Magazine, February, 2009

TELLIER AND BRUNELLE FAMILY TREE

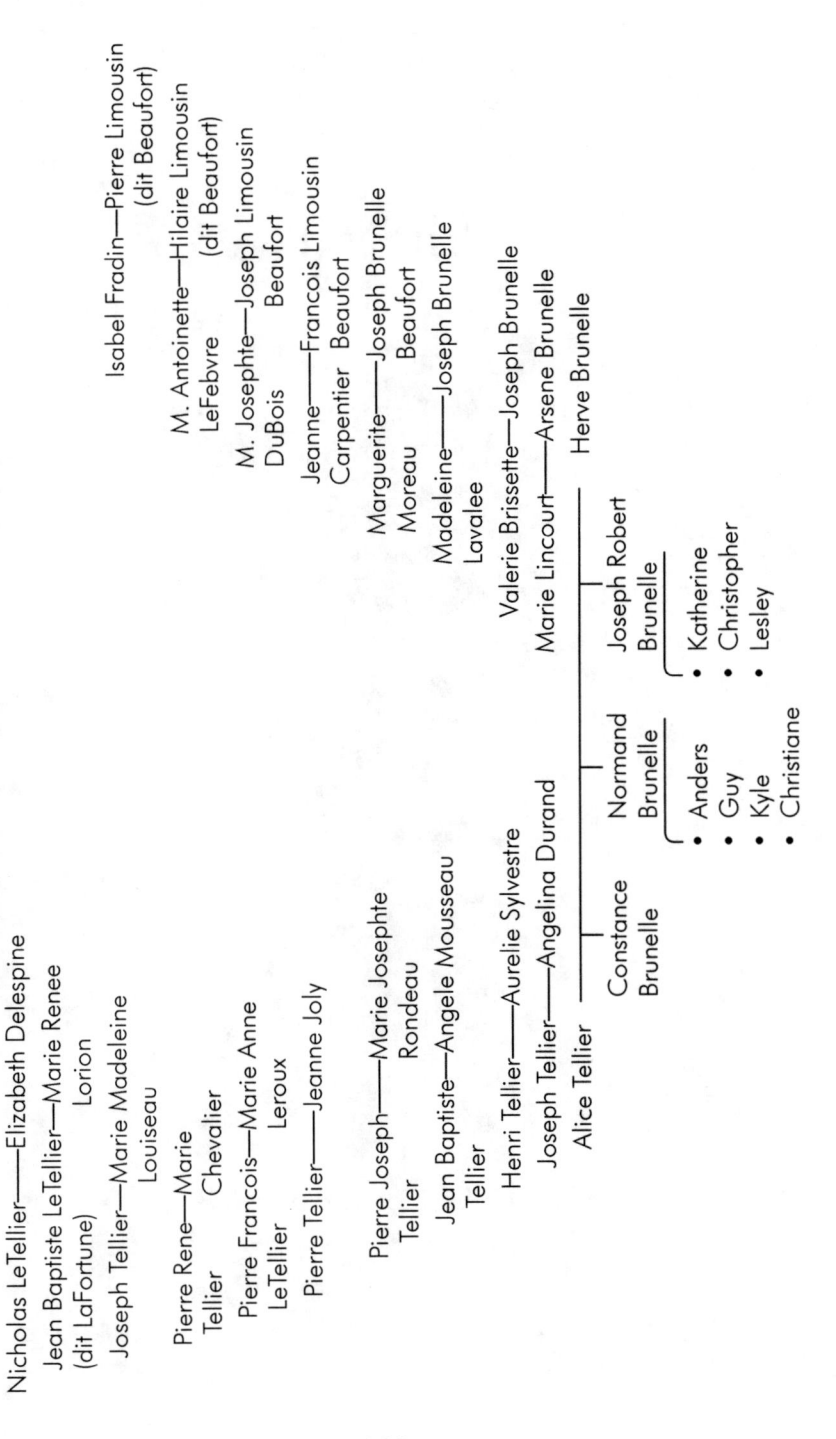

Nicholas LeTellier——Elizabeth Delespine

Jean Baptiste LeTellier——Marie Renee
(dit LaFortune)　　　　　Lorion

Joseph Tellier——Marie Madeleine
　　　　　　　　　Louiseau

Pierre Rene——Marie
Tellier　　　　Chevalier

Pierre Francois——Marie Anne
LeTellier　　　　　Leroux

Pierre Tellier——Jeanne Joly

Pierre Joseph——Marie Josephte
Tellier　　　　　Rondeau

Jean Baptiste——Angele Mousseau
Tellier

Henri Tellier——Aurelie Sylvestre

Joseph Tellier——Angelina Durand

Alice Tellier

　　　　　　　　　　　　　Isabel Fradin——Pierre Limousin
　　　　　　　　　　　　　　　　　　　　　(dit Beaufort)

　　　　　　　　　M. Antoinette——Hilaire Limousin
　　　　　　　　　LeFebvre　　　　　(dit Beaufort)

　　　　　　　　M. Josephte——Joseph Limousin
　　　　　　　　DuBois　　　　　Beaufort

　　　　　　Jeanne——Francois Limousin
　　　　　　Carpentier　Beaufort

　　　　Marguerite——Joseph Brunelle
　　　　Moreau　　　　Beaufort

　　　Madeleine——Joseph Brunelle
　　　Lavalee

　　Valerie Brissette——Joseph Brunelle

　　Marie Lincourt——Arsene Brunelle

　　　　　　Herve Brunelle

Constance　Normand　Joseph Robert
Brunelle　　Brunelle　Brunelle

　　　　　　• Anders　　• Katherine
　　　　　　• Guy　　　　• Christopher
　　　　　　• Kyle　　　　• Lesley
　　　　　　• Christiane

183

PHOTOGRAPHS

French Soldier Circa 1660s

Fort Michillimackinac (Mackinaw City MI) replica. Top left and bottom show
St. Anne's church, site of marriage of Jean Baptiste Tellier in 1747. Top
right shows gate house with soldier.

Fort Michillimackinac

Exterior and interior views of Church of St. Cuthbert located in St. Cutnbert, Quebec, Canada circa 2001.

Exterior & interior views of Church of St. Cuthbert

Manville Brass Band circa 1900. Arsene Brunelle 2nd row, 2nd from left

Manville Brass Band

Arsene & Marie Brunelle Family circa 1916. First Row: Arsene, Angeline, Eugene, Marie. Back Row: Bertha, Emile, Harvey, Tony, Helen, Romeo

Arsene & Marie Brunelle family

Joseph and Angelina Tellier family 1907. Front row: Joseph, Alice, Rose, Annette. Middle: Diana. Back row: Marie Louise, Napoleon, Alphonse, Marion, Philbert

Joseph & Angelina Tellier family

Alice Tellier, age 4, 1907

Alice Tellier

Left Alice, Father Demaros, 2 friends

Left Alice, 6 friends

Alice front row, right

Alice second from right

Left Alice

Left Alice Alice back row, right
Alice Tellier with friends from St Ann's church, Woonsocket RI, circa 1915-1920

Alice Tellier with friends

Diana's grave 2001

Alice Tellier at Diana's grave
Circa 1920

Diana circa 1917

Funeral card 16 Oct 1919
Diana deceased at 20 yrs,
2 months, 6 days

Diana circa 1917

Collage of Diana Tellier

Collage of Diana Tellier

Workers leaving Manville Mill circa 1900

Workers leaving Manville Mill

Romeo Brunelle in Army band uniform
Circa 1917

Romeo Brunelle in Army Uniform
Circa 1917

Romeo Brunelle in Army uniform

uilding that housed the Alice Mill of Woonsocket Rubber Co
Photo 1998

Alice Mill

Woonsocket Armory where Alice and Harvey met.
Photo 1998

Woonsocket Armory

Left to right:
Mr. & Mrs. Tellier
Alice, Harvey
Mr. & Mrs. Brunelle

Wedding Day
July 7, 1924
Woonsocket RI

Left to right:
Joseph Tellier
Marie Brunelle
Alice Brunelle
Harvey Brunelle

25th Anniversary
July 1949
Manville RI

Harvey & Alice

50th Anniversary
July 1974
Long Island City NY

Collage of marriage & anniversaries of Harvey & Alice Brunelle

Collage of marriage & anniversaries of Harvey & Alice Brunelle

Advertisement for Chrysler touring car

Normand Brunelle age 4 yrs on his father's 1929 Chrysler.

Normand Brunelle age 4 yrs on on his grandfather's 1925 Chrysler.

Chrysler autos

198

Arsene Brunelle family home
Circa 1920

Brunelle Long Island City home
Circa 1990

Former Arsene
Brunelle family
home Circa 1980

Brunelle family homes

Circa 1955: Normand & Nancy Brunelle.

1945: Nancy Mattson & Normand Brunelle

Circa 1962
Normand Brunelle family:
Left to right
Kyle, Nancy, Anders, Normand, Guy

Normand & Nancy Brunelle

Woonsocket RI
Circa 1948

Left to Right:
Bob Brunelle
Ernest Villeneuve
Tom Gil
Connie Brunelle Gil
Normand Brunelle

Bob Brunelle
Long Island City   1952

Bob Brunelle
K-13 Korea
1952

Bob Brunelle collage

Providence RI 1987. Front: Alice Tellier Brunelle, Sue Brunelle
Back: Marta & Bob Brunelle, Cecile Tellier Dubeau, Connie
Brunelle Gil, Ernest Villeneuve, Helen Brunelle, Vivian Brunelle

Long Island City NY circa 1990. Lesley Brunelle, Christopher Brunelle, Kathy Brunelle Milom

Providence family picture & Long Island City family picture

Harvey and Alice Brunelle
Long Island City
Circa 1960

Alice Brunelle with
grandchild and great
grandchildren
New Berlin NY circa 1993

back: Katherine & Jessica
middle: Melissa & Alice
front: Jacqueline & Amanda

**Harvey & Alice Brunelle in Long Island City
& Alice with grandchildren**

Montreal, Canada, August 1926: Villeneuve family with Brother Andre at St. Joseph's Oratory. Left to right: Eddie, Ernest and their father. Front center: Brother Andre

Woonsocket RI 1998. Ernest Villeneuve and Bob Brunelle

**Montreal, Canada - Villeneuve family
& Woonsocket RI - Ernest & Bob**

New Berlin NY Summer 2003. Back row: Keith Hellin, Middle: Melissa Milom, Marta Brunelle, Kathy and Cody Hellin,   Jessica Milom, Front: Jacqueline Milom, Amanda Milom, Molly (the dog)

"Cousins" New Berlin NY   2003
Left to right: Gene Peloquin, Bob Brunelle, Rene Tellier

New Berlin summer 2003 & cousins 2003

Guy & Patricia Brunelle
August 18, 2002

Anders & Felix "Maruja" Brunelle
November 11, 2007

Kyle & Deborah Brunelle   April 24, 2003

Brunelle family wedding photos

Guy & Patti Brunelle's children: Left to right: Colette, Bianca, Adrien.   Family dog: Jasmine   2007

Alice Brunelle's 101st birthday, June 4, 2004, Long Island City
Rear: Guy Brunelle. Middle: Connie Brunelle Gil, Normand Brunelle
Chris Brunelle, Anders Brunelle. Front: Bianca Brunelle,
Alice Brunelle

Guy & Patti Brunelle children
& Alice Brunelle's 101st birthday

Manassas VA, September 2008

Front: Melissa Milom
Row 2: Jessica & Amanda Milom
Row 3: Jacqueline Milom
Row 4: Kathy Hellin and
       Bob Brunelle

"First Day of School"   September 2008   Cody Hellin

Manassas VA Sept. 2008 & first day of school

Glen Cove, NY August 2008. Christiane & Kevin Murphy family.
Children left to right: James, Mary, Luke, Kevin, Katherine

Berlin, Germany, April 2009. left to right: Shirley Niles,
Birgitta Petersson, Chris Brunelle

Glen Cove August 2008 & Berlin, Germany, April 2009